Studies on the principle of sharing

Mohammed Sofiane Mesbahi

First edition

Copyright © 2020 Mohammed Sofiane Mesbahi

The moral right of the author has been asserted.

Apart from any fair dealing for the purposes of research or private study, or criticism or review, as permitted under the Copyright, Designs and Patents Act 1988, this publication may only be reproduced, stored or transmitted, in any form or by any means, with the prior permission in writing of the publishers, or in the case of reprographic reproduction in accordance with the terms of licences issued by the Copyright Licensing Agency. Enquiries concerning reproduction outside those terms should be sent to the publishers.

Cover artwork: Nicholas Roerich (1874 – 1947). Kanchenjunga, 1936.
Courtesy of Nicholas Roerich Museum, New York.
With special thanks to Meryl Tihanyi for assistance with the cover design.

Matador
9 Priory Business Park,
Wistow Road, Kibworth Beauchamp,
Leicestershire. LE8 0RX
Tel: 0116 279 2299
Email: books@troubador.co.uk
Web: www.troubador.co.uk/matador
Twitter: @matadorbooks

ISBN 978 1800461 062

British Library Cataloguing in Publication Data.
A catalogue record for this book is available from the British Library.

Printed and bound in Great Britain by 4edge Limited
Typeset in 11pt Adobe Garamond Pro by Troubador Publishing Ltd, Leicester, UK

Matador is an imprint of Troubador Publishing Ltd

ALSO BY THE AUTHOR

Heralding Article 25: A people's strategy for world transformation

The intersection of politics and spirituality in addressing the climate crisis

Towards a universal basic income for all humanity

The young disciple: Sir, what is the relationship that exists between truth, silence and nothingness?

The man from the Far East: Shall we find out together and meditate upon this question till sunrise?

The young disciple: Yes, yes of course.

As the sun started to rise, the man from the Far East opened His eyes and observed the young disciple for a long moment, then asked: What was yesterday's question?

The young disciple (with eyes shut): I don't remember. Can we keep meditating till nightfall?

The man from the Far East smiled affectionately at the young disciple, then vanished into thin air.

Contents

Editor's preface	IX
The cry for justice	1
Commercialisation: the antithesis of sharing	17
Uniting the people of the world	35
A discourse on beliefs, ideologies and 'isms'	59
An enquiry into the meaning of sharing food	87
Rise up America, rise up!	111
Christmas, the system and I	133
About the author	161

Editor's preface

These seven articles were originally published over the course of 2011 to 2014, during the momentous revolutionary period that followed the global financial crisis. Much of the writing speaks to that sudden democratic awakening of society, when public uprisings and mass occupations became a significant force for change on the world stage. But the essential vision contained within these pages goes far beyond that single historical moment and has even greater relevance and urgency today.

Each article or 'study' reads like a joint enquiry between author and reader, leading us both to investigate the meaning of sharing as a solution to world problems—not only in an economic sense but also from social, psychological and even spiritual perspectives. The book can be read as a series of self-contained and separate commentaries, or as interlinked chapters that explicate the repeated themes from many angles.

One theme Mesbahi constantly returns to is Article 25 of the Universal Declaration of Human Rights. First adopted by the United Nations General Assembly in 1948, this upholds everyone's right to an adequate standard of living—including food, housing, healthcare and social security. Finally guaranteeing these basic entitlements for all people is central to our vision at Share The World's Resources (STWR), informing our wider educational and campaigning work as a civil society organisation. The collected writings in this book help to elucidate that immense, all-embracing vision which also underpins Mesbahi's later works—particularly our flagship publication, *Heralding Article 25: A people's strategy for world transformation*.

What you are about to read should not be considered a volume of academic essays. Perhaps it is better described as an inspirational teaching for how to bring about a more inclusive, just and equal world. By repeatedly focusing on the need for people to unite through unceasing demonstrations on behalf of the world's majority poor, we are also called to participate in this great planetary endeavour ourselves. For as Mesbahi makes clear: 'Without this vital missing factor in modern world affairs, there is no other way out of the critical impasse that faces humanity in the short years ahead.'

London, UK, September 2020

THE CRY FOR JUSTICE

Originally published on sharing.org, December 2011

If only one tear is shed for others out of compassion, life in its eternity will speak about your loving heart to all the stars that you can see.

All the commentary from expert analysts about the melting financial system give almost no insight into what is really happening in the world today. Countless articles are written about how to fix the economy and restore growth to the system, but they are only relevant to a system that was never sustainable and is now coming to an end. What we call 'the system' has become so complicated that it appears to have a life of its own, and not even the most sophisticated economist understands what is going on anymore. Few policymakers speak in terms that mean anything to the ordinary person who is struggling to find or keep a job, make ends meet and provide for their family. The disconnection between the worlds of powerful politicians in their private meetings and the everyday lives of the people they are called to serve is more apparent than ever before. But at the same time, something profoundly new is happening throughout the world that requires a much simpler way of looking at things if we are to comprehend what is taking place.

The protests arising in almost every country are a magnificent sight, but it is important to recognise that every one of us who participates in protests against 'the system' is also implicated in the mess created by bankers and politicians. Without exception, we are all part of the system. Unless we recognise that society is an extension of ourselves, our protests could lead to tremendous chaos and violence as the economic situation continues to worsen, while political parties of both left and right fail to provide an answer to increasing social problems and inequalities. The system is made up of ordinary people like you and me, of men and women with families and children, which is why it is imperative not to attack 'the system' when this would be tantamount to going against each other.

In modern history many governments have tried, with good intentions, to completely change the system. This change was always imposed on the basis of a political ideology, but the time has come when ideologies are not needed any more. There was nothing inherently wrong with the principles underlying capitalism, socialism and communism, but governments abused these principles with an imposing and arrogant attitude towards their people in the name of a belief. Today, more and more people are becoming conscious of the need to be free from these political 'isms' that have caused so much suffering and conflict throughout the world. More than a decade after the new millennium it should appear inane to call oneself a communist, a socialist or a capitalist, or to believe that freedom can be acquired through wearing a uniform—in other words, that we can destroy one ideology by replacing it with another.

Witnessing the uprisings and demonstrations that are now taking place, we could say in a literal sense that people are becoming more aware. Without any condescension, this is one way to put it—that more and more people are starting to think for themselves, and are no longer relying on what other people tell them to think, are no longer 'believing in a belief'. Our education systems do not help us to understand that ideologies are a denial of human freedom; they do not teach us what it means to be free within. But today, people are realising this intuitively for themselves. Hence all the changes that are happening so dramatically across the world.

Please observe the so-called Arab Spring; millions of people courageously freed themselves from dictators who had imposed beliefs and ideologies on their people for decades, but now that the revolution has unfolded many different factions are trying to impose all manner of new beliefs upon each other. In Egypt, the army quickly tried to rebuild the old system based on power and privilege even when a million people again took to the streets. In Zucotti Park and at St Paul's, as in any mass protest movement, there were also many intellectual factions with different beliefs all combating for attention within the crowd. Let us not be fooled. Democracy is closely related to freedom, but the kind of democracies we have today are an imposed and controlling form of social organisation. We will only know the true meaning of democracy when each and every one of us experiences the freedom that comes from within, and not before. At the very least, it is not enough to vote for a political party once every few years when no leading politician has an answer to our social and economic problems.

As we stand with the new movement of protestors, we must look closely at what it means when we cry for justice. There are many stories now being reported about the rich people who are accumulating wealth in the midst of economic austerity, which of course leads to rightful anger against bankers and the unbridled greed that has been sanctified in modern-day society. But which is the greater sin: the banker's bonus, or the fact that thousands of people are dying from hunger each day in a world of plenty? The global economy is sinking and so the people's voice is rising, but why are there no demonstrations in our city squares when people are dying from hunger?

It is because we do not see the interconnection between our different lives. We have not been educated to see the very poorest people as our brothers and sisters, or to see the world as an interdependent whole. A child is not taught how to be in touch with himself, with his own nature, but is rather conditioned in how to become a 'somebody' in a dysfunctional society based on competition and stress. In universities we may study many books about the history of human civilization, philosophy, politics, the arts and so on, but we are not taught in the simplest human terms how to serve other people. The consequence, in a global and collective sense, is that we do not understand that we are one humanity, that we are all dependent upon each other, and that we have a responsibility to care for those less fortunate than ourselves.

The protests erupting in Wall Street and elsewhere could have happened a long, long time ago. So why now, all of a sudden? Because millions of people in the affluent countries are beginning to feel the pinch. Even when we cannot pay our mortgages, however unjust the circumstances, why don't we think about those who are poorer than ourselves? There are many different levels of poverty, and as we know in the USA and other rich countries there are an extraordinary number of people living in relative poverty—but how about the kind of poverty when you cannot find enough food for you or your children to eat? When you do not have shelter, or money, or even the most basic form of healthcare to prevent you from dying? We are all familiar with the phrase 'a crime against humanity', but why doesn't the international community ascribe this phrase to the thousands of people dying from hunger each day, or to the 1.4 billion people that the World Bank cursorily describes as 'the extreme poor'?[1]

Now that the economic system is collapsing, every nation has to begin to restructure itself, and we can all play a part in this process. But we have to understand that this begins with ending hunger. We cannot even look at the word injustice without first looking at the problem of hunger. It is as if we have bought a new home, but first we must clean up the mess left by the old tenants. That mess is the problem of hunger. We cannot go out into the world and campaign for justice for ourselves when our own children are waiting at home, abandoned by us and hungry. The world is in a state of disrepair and requires a dramatic process of rehabilitation, but first we have to look after our own children, who are the hungry people of the world.

After 9-11 happened, a huge army was sent to Iraq over land, sea and air within a month. Notwithstanding the terrible consequences of that illegal war, just imagine if all that manpower and expertise was redirected to giving life, not taking life away? Imagine if the world's military resources were mobilised to eradicate hunger as a foremost priority—above geopolitics, defence or corporate profit. Recently, NATO sent hundreds of millions of dollars effectively flying through the air to stop Gaddafi from massacring his own people.[2] Whether or not we agree that this was a necessary action, there is another question we should ask: why doesn't NATO send all their planes and armies into Africa to help feed the people?

Many more people in Benghazi may have died without outside intervention, but at the same time thousands of people were dying from hunger and poverty in other parts of the world, and continue to die each day. Why doesn't NATO prevent Al-Shabab from diverting aid away from the Somalian people?[3] We all know the answer: because there is no strategic or economic interest for them there. But this is not a cause that motivates people to protest *en masse* in the streets, demanding an answer from our governments: 'Why don't we help the hungry millions?'

Even the church has failed in its duty to shake the world's conscience about the blasphemy of hunger, despite there being no cardinal rule to prevent the clergy from demonstrating in our city squares for freedom from want. When protesters camped outside St Paul's Cathedral in London, many banners posed the question 'What would Jesus do?' We might wonder how the church would respond if Christ were to reappear today as a 'divine activist' moving among the mass rallies for freedom and justice across the world. Unfortunately, when we label the very few people who attempt to do the right thing for the world as 'activists', we infer that an activist is somehow different and set apart from the ordinary citizen. The media and advertising industry encourage us to adopt such labels, which enable us to separate our social identities and not feel connected to the suffering and vast inequity that plagues the earth. It is these same divisions in our consciousness that allow us to say: 'There has always been hunger, and always will be'. Or to nod our head at the warnings of environmentalists, and then to say: 'But it is naive to believe that we can change the world'. In this sense, the word activist really means 'the one whom nobody listens to'.

An understanding of justice also requires awareness, which means to see things clearly, to think for oneself, to not have a belief in a belief. Now that the old order is collapsing and no government knows what to do, we can no longer point the finger at our politicians alone. We like to say 'it's the fault of my government', but are we not also to blame for the world situation through our own lack of action and our complacency? As we have seen in the Middle East, when two million people stand in the street and peacefully shake their fists the government has no choice but to listen or leave office.

*

Let us try and understand, in the simplest terms, what this means for the economist and the politician. Since it is obvious that our economic, social and political systems need to be totally restructured, the correct responsibility of governments is to redesign these systems specifically so that no-one dies of hunger. In the first instance, this requires international cooperation for an emergency program of redistribution unlike anything we have seen before. Such a program cannot be based on charity, which has absolutely nothing to do with justice. Charity is of course critical in the kind of world we have today where billions of people are suffering in poverty, but the necessity of charity is a sad representation of public complacency. An emergency program cannot be based on the existing premise of 'let's do our best to feed the starving people', but must rather be initiated with the understanding that 'this should never happen again'.

There is plenty of food and resources to feed, clothe, house and care for everyone in the world, as long stipulated as a human right in Article 25 of the Universal Declaration.[4] This Article, which is the expression of justice in its strictest sense, must become the law for every nation. Just as there are laws to obey when a country joins the European Community, the human rights articles of the United Nations must *legally* obligate member states to collectively prevent any person dying from hunger in any country. Article 25 must be translated into the rule of law, backed up by the force of public opinion around the world. The voice of the people should be heard and represented in the United Nations—that is what the United Nations is for. It should come to represent the heart and minds of the people. This will inevitably take a long time, and each nation should continue to grow within its own traditions. But as a very first step, enlightened politicians and the public should voice their demand for an emergency redistribution program to be initiated under the aegis of the United Nations General Assembly, which should become the most important work that the United Nations has ever undertaken.

The logistical details of such a program will be an immense challenge for governments to negotiate and plan, but there can be no gainsaying its broad mandate. Again and again we see humanitarian emergencies with the same old story, as in Turkey's earthquake recently or the floods in Thailand: not enough resources, not enough support, not enough aid to go around. Even in the richest country with the largest military, people in New Orleans were left to fend for themselves in the aftermath of Hurricane Katrina, calling out to the world 'Where's President Bush?' When we want to protect our own interests or go to war, everything happens so quickly—we have all the equipment, all the weapons, all the manpower, all the money. But when it comes to the suffering of poor people, all of a sudden money is non-existent. This is the trend that must be reversed. This is why the prevention of human deprivation, whatever its cause—poverty, conflict or natural disaster—must be guaranteed by an international authority. Think of it like a worldwide emergency services, funded by contributions from every nation. We should not even consider this to be a 'humanitarian' operation, which has connotations too similar to charity. Rather, these programs should be permanently structured into our reformed global governance institutions and enshrined in international law.

None of this will happen without an unparalleled uprising of public support. A solution to the world's problems cannot be brought about by any political party or ideology, and can only happen through a free, united and single voice of the people of the world. Ideologies and belief systems have no further part to play in the changes that lie ahead. A healthy revolution in fact begins with the act of wanting to be free of all 'isms' and ideologies that constantly harass human free will and prevent us from demonstrating love between people of every race and culture. To be free from beliefs and ideologies will naturally allow our minds the space to know ourselves, which in turn will give us the ability, the energy and the love to identify ourselves with others.

But it is futile to become 'anti' any belief or ideology, such as to stand against capitalism. It is time to put capitalism in its right place and redistribute the world's resources to where they are needed most. Capitalism came very naturally to us—it is natural to say 'this is yours, and this is mine', but the time is coming when we must say 'let's share what we have'. Sharing means 'to be with', because we cannot share with another person without silently acknowledging that we are together, that we are here to help one another. In this sense, the principle of sharing has the intrinsic propensity to unite and not divide.

The beauty of sharing is that it does not belong to any political party or 'ism', but to the people of the world. It doesn't belong to the socialist party, or the communists, or anyone else. It is the freeing agent from a painful history of ideologies and beliefs that have caused such tremendous conflicts with each other. When we understand that the principle of sharing is fundamental to our survival but tragically neglected at every level of society, we will recognise that sharing is the surest guide to justice and peace. Then we will each know ourselves as an ambassador for humanity, because above all nations is the united people of the world.

What could this mean for the people protesting in New York and every other city? These protesters know very well that we need to redistribute wealth, that we need to stop money from going through the wrong hands—to the arms industry in particular. Whichever way you look at it, war must now come to an end. Nobody wants war anymore—or rather, no country can afford to go to war anymore as the world economy continues to melt and collapse. The protesters are also very aware that there is more than enough money to go around, but that it is hoarded by powerful families and corporations, even by the governments who spend it injudiciously. So each nation has to redistribute its wealth and resources more fairly among its own population.

But we also need to redistribute resources globally, initially on an emergency basis to all people who are without the basic necessities of life, and eventually through new international economic arrangements no longer based on competition and material gain. These longer-term transformations will require visionary thinking and a new kind of economist, and it may take many years to restructure our global governance systems. Through the sharing of world resources, laws will have to change by the shovel; everything will need to be simplified. This is why we should not waste our time listening to the advice of the orthodox economist or establishment politician, as their theories are outdated and irrelevant to the coming era. When the principle of sharing begins to influence government policy, the present economic system will naturally change or melt away. Both cannot coexist, for one is divisive in its complexity and the other is unifying in its simplicity.

No-one is immune from the changes that lie ahead, so let us not work against the system, but together let's transform it. This requires an attitude of confidence that we really can transform the system, and that a better world is possible. And this requires awareness, and togetherness, and more and more perseverance—especially perseverance. As we have seen, governments instinctively abhor any uprising of the people because their power is soon put in jeopardy, so their tactic through the police is to discourage even the most peaceful form of protest. So we have to carry on and on, otherwise change is impossible.

We are already becoming a powerful force, structuring ourselves and becoming organised into one voice. Every demonstration around the world should express, in its own creative way, a refusal to carry on living as before. But we cannot change the world without first looking after the most vulnerable people, which means that we have to demand from our governments an immediate end to hunger, everywhere. A true social revolution has to have morality at its heart, which is why an end to life-threatening deprivation in every country must become our first priority. The key is for everyone to raise their voice for greater economic sharing, and to continually push the boundaries of our demands until governments implement this unifying principle into world affairs. Now is the time, as it always has been.

COMMERCIALISATION: THE ANTITHESIS OF SHARING

Originally published on sharing.org, April 2014

The greatest danger in the world today is not commercialisation per se but our constant identification with its inner and outer manifestation, whereby human intelligence is led in the opposite direction from nature and spiritual evolution.

'Sharing is the key to solving the world's problems.' Such a statement is so simple that it may fail to make an appeal, so we must go much deeper into this subject if we want to comprehend what this means. In order to understand how sharing is the surest guide to justice, peace and right human relations, we need to investigate its meaning and significance from many angles—including psychologically and spiritually, as well as from a social, economic and political perspective. There are myriad ways to look at sharing because the nature of this principle is a powerhouse within the Laws of Life, and anyone can intuit and experience its extraordinary versatility. But if it is true that sharing is fundamentally important for our continued evolution on this earth, then the first question we need to examine is: why isn't this principle understood as an answer to the crisis of our civilisation?

One way to find out how sharing has been subverted in our societies is to observe how commercialisation has increasingly structured itself into our consciousness. It is easy to say that sharing is the solution to the world's ills, but this assertion becomes merely another lofty belief unless we also consider how commercialisation is tightening its grip on our evolution by the hour. To find the key to solving the problems of humanity, we must also ask ourselves why we have allowed the authority of the politician to dominate our social and economic arrangements, our education and our everyday lives. Most importantly, we also need to examine, through self-reflection and inner awareness, how our complacency and wrong education has led to a collective indifference to the suffering of others.

We all understand what sharing means on a personal level, as everybody shares within their homes and communities. So why do so few people understand the need to implement the principle of sharing on a national and worldwide level? A large part of the answer to this question can be simply put: it is because the foundations of our societies have been constructed in such a way that market forces have been given too much free reign, and effectively let loose. We have developed complex economic and political systems that are increasingly geared towards profit and commercialisation—the tax structures, the large corporations, the countless legal regulations that are created to defend private interests. All of this creates an extremely complicated and divisive society. Nobody understands the system in the end, but the system understands precisely how to manipulate us for its own purposes. And in such a complex society, with so many laws and policies created to facilitate commercialisation, the principle of sharing is almost non-existent.

As long as we live in a society that is driven by profit and commercialisation, the principle of sharing will always be eclipsed. In every sphere of human activity it can be observed that when commercialisation moves in, sharing moves out. The same reality also pertains to the environment: when commercialisation moves in, nature moves out. Indeed, when commercialisation moves in it can be so invasive, so destructive, that it can break apart families. It can break apart traditions and national identities, as we have seen with many free trade agreements and the economic integration of Europe. Wherever these forces are unleashed it can lead to a widening gulf between rich and poor, a contagion of spiritual turmoil, and ultimately a diversion of man's God-given intelligence in the opposite direction of social progress and evolution.

We are not talking about commerce *per se*, but about the greed and selfishness that is involved when market forces are let loose, and the complacency and indifference that is the result. It doesn't mean that we have to work in commerce for this to apply to us—it applies to us all, because we all live in a world that is permeated by market forces. The danger is not even the process of commercialisation as an economic phenomenon, but rather our constant identification with its inner and outer manifestation.

There is no use in trying to grasp or define commercialisation in psychological terms, because we cannot understand the malefic forces that underpin its processes from a dictionary definition. The old understanding of commerce as simply buying and selling has almost been lost because, from a certain perspective, market forces have infiltrated our cells like a disease and transmuted into a silent killer called commercialisation. It is part of us and living within us. Commercialisation is the system we have created in relationship to the earth and to each other, and it is inherent in the movement of people and life within society. Of course, there is nothing wrong with the systematic exchanging of goods and services within or between nations. But just as a knife can be used to cut vegetables or to kill people, so can commerce be used for good or ill.

Our enquiry therefore concerns how commercialisation has misled our creativity from fulfilling the simple needs that we all have in common, and skewed our motives towards the mindless pursuit of profit and endless consumption. Why do we fail to recognise, and therefore restrict, the destructive power of commercialisation despite all the harm that it is wreaking upon society and the environment? A response to this question can also be simply put: it is because we are all searching for happiness. And commercialisation is very clever in promising us happiness, a 'good life', a more comfortable life and security. We are all searching for security. But it is a false sense of security that we are being sold—a dangerous fantasy.

Again, we are not talking about security in a solely material sense, such as the kind of economic security that a family needs for bread and shelter. Our deeper concern here is the search for psychological security that ultimately drives us to become more isolated from each other, and essentially denies our intelligence and freedom. It is the need for psychological security that impels us to constantly search for the personal delusion that we call happiness. And the forces of commercialisation are expert in offering us happiness by misdirecting our minds from awareness of the inner Self, which is the only place where any real contentment or joy can be found.

Happiness in the context of a highly commercialised and inequitable society is one of the ugliest social fantasies that we are attached to, because in such a society happiness can only exist alongside misery and sorrow. Like a sink, it always comes with two taps: the hot and the cold. Happiness and misery in a dysfunctional society inevitably exist side by side. The yearning for an illusory form of happiness can also be dangerous, however, when in that process we become emotionally trapped and self-absorbed, and our lives become imitative and uncreative. Before long, our natural tendency to love and empathise with those less fortunate than ourselves can be overridden by complacency, indifference and fear. Which leaves us with an important question: what is the relationship that exists between fear and the search for personal happiness?

The ability to look at oneself inwardly without fear is swiftly abducted by the forces of commercialisation. Even in our closest personal relationships we live in fear as a result of our continuous search for happiness and security, which is how commercialisation infiltrates our minds and manipulates us psychologically. It creates endless desires for objects and possessions, and it places a limit within our consciousness so that we do not see beyond our emotional attachments. It can reduce us to queuing all night long for the latest fad or gadget, and it is capable of putting us into a trance until we think that shopping is our religion, or that the profoundest meaning of common sense is 'buy one, get one free'. It can lead a person to look at a prospective partner and think: 'They are good looking, but do they have any money?' Or it can induce the teenager to copy their schoolmates and aspire to be like them too, to wear the ever-changing fashions and flaunt the expensive 'look'. It is very easy for commercialisation to manipulate the brains of young children, and to distort the true meaning of education—which really concerns inner freedom and self-knowledge, not conformity, comparison or competition. Commercialisation makes us small, it makes us afraid, it degrades our humility, and we are not even aware of it. These forces have built into our minds such conditioning and fear that the simple way of sharing no longer makes an appeal, leading to mental blindness of the highest order.

Observe the basic psychological dynamic that is structured into our consciousness by commercialisation: constant measurement and comparison between different people, and the instinctive worshipping of success. The desire to 'make it', to become a 'somebody'. And the same adulation of success and achievement is ingrained in our children from the youngest age, to make them want to look at themselves in the mirror one day and say: 'I made it'. Even the artist strives to say 'I achieved', or desires others to say of him: 'You know that man? He achieved so much'. But when we define ourselves in relation to others, when we constantly measure and compare ourselves with others who have what we don't have, we end up creating a peculiar complex of inferiority that hinders the expression of our spiritual potential and right human relations. This dynamic suits the forces of commercialisation very well. Because in our continued worshipping of success and achievement, we thereby sustain the corrosive influence of profit and materiality in every area of our lives—in our schools, in our workplaces, in our homes, even in our dreams.

Imagine if a famous celebrity or a billionaire were brought into the room now, and how your attitude towards that person would be very different from normal. Because we are like that too, we are also conditioned to think: 'Become successful, then you are a somebody'. We are all impelled through social conditioning to inwardly bow to the authority of a 'somebody', which is essentially how commercialisation creates machines out of people. Its first job is to make us believe that success is the way, but to achieve success we are told that we have to work very hard, that we have to achieve. Then we learn that to achieve we have to compete with everyone else, that we have to become a 'winner'. It is not long before we have lost our inborn freedom and creativity, before we begin to follow ideologies and beliefs, before we conform and become complacent.

This is the inevitable outcome of worshipping success and achievement: our complacency and indifference to the suffering of others. Because this is what the obsession with individual achievement in our societies does—it breeds indifference. So even the highly educated person who we would call reasonably-minded—a respectable, morally-upright citizen—will casually say 'there has always been hunger, and there always will be'.

Furthermore, it is curious to notice the obscure emotional effect that commercialisation has on the person who looks at this unfortunate planet and says: 'I want to help, but I feel so helpless'. No doubt there is always something we can do to help alleviate the suffering of the world, but it is largely the forces of commercialisation that lead us to feel overwhelmed, separated and helpless as individuals. The unchaining of market forces in every department of human life is gradually taking away our goodwill, taking away our compassion, taking away our awareness and our common sense. These same forces have bullied the principle of sharing with all their might over recent decades, growing in such an elusive and refined way that to be complacent is now the norm.

Thus it is no exaggeration to say that commercialisation is the *bête noire* of human evolution, or like an invisible tsunami that slowly deluges all levels and aspects of society. Anyone who believes in the devil should think again about who and what that is, if such a thing exists. What is evil, after all, without our freely chosen identification with its manifestation? Our complacency and wrong education has turned commercialisation into a powerful hammer, while the principle of sharing is a miniscule nail—meaning it's a way of life to know that people are dying from hunger in other parts of the world, while we ourselves do nothing about it.

Not that we can excuse our complacency and indifference. Our complacency should be taken to court where we should all be judged for committing crimes against humanity. We should form a planetary queue outside the International Criminal Court in The Hague, because we are all complicit. Through our collective complacency and indifference, we have remained silent while the earth was being pillaged and destroyed, and we have looked the other way while our brothers and sisters are dying in poverty. In the final analysis, the people who desecrated the earth and those who did nothing to stop them are one and the same, because one cannot exist without the other. We could even say that the one who looks the other way is even more culpable, because the one who is hoarding the world's resources and destroying the earth is entirely dependent on the complacency of others—he could not do it otherwise.

In truth, commercialisation is nothing less than a silent war, a war against humanity's growth and evolution. This statement cannot be emphasised strongly enough: commercialisation is a *war*. Not just a war between different sides, between competing nations or rival tribes, but a war in itself. It is a war that is being waged within every household, community and nation because commercialisation is so devious, so intelligent, that it precisely knows the weaknesses of humanity. It knows our emotional nature intimately well because this is where it resides, and from where it manipulates us. And from there it fuses with our beliefs and ideologies, and fosters different factions, and feeds off the political parties fighting one another. It is so subtle that it is able to buy stocks and shares in our beliefs and isms, for this is where it invests in order to grow.

The hidden reality is that for several decades another Auschwitz is slowly being built, although this time in a different form by driving humanity to fully capitulate to the forces of commercialisation. Global warfare today is not only being waged in the form of tanks and guns, but also through the destruction that is concealed in the creed of market forces that has gradually overshadowed every nation of the world. Who can deny that thousands of deaths from needless poverty-related causes is not already the equivalent of an Auschwitz that occurs every single day? As the economic situation deteriorates further in different countries, as the world's stock markets continue to roar and then collapse, the forces of commercialisation are becoming ever more triumphant in bringing about conflict, chaos and life-threatening extremes of inequality. The minority rich are becoming ever richer, and the majority poor are becoming even poorer, until a worldwide Auschwitz could increasingly take the form of massive deaths due to poverty and hunger. A great, silent war is being fought on every plane of our existence which the men and women of goodwill throughout the world are only just beginning to sense, even if unconsciously. How we respond to this emergency on Planet Earth will determine the future prospects for the human race. The reader is urged to think very carefully for themselves over what has just been said.

*

The following points summarise only some of the veiled, pervasive and extremely dangerous effects on humanity of rampant commercialisation that:

» sustains mind conditioning which is pollution to the soul

- » creates and deepens a complex of inferiority in people wherever they are, leading a person to believe they must become a certain 'somebody', thereby losing their true spiritual purpose in life
- » instils an unconscious and often life-lasting sense of psychological fear in people's minds that prevents any curiosity or open-mindedness about the spiritual meaning of life, and ensures that complacency is sustained at all times
- » constantly misdirects people's attention in order to inhibit awareness of the inner Self and the moment of now during daily life, and throughout the course of a lifetime
- » drives individuals and groups to be caught in all manner of beliefs, and out of those beliefs the manifold isms are nourished and perpetuated
- » prevents people from being creative, communicative and giving in society
- » weakens social services
- » produces a separation between citizens and the state, leading to the sporadic eruption of chaos and riots
- » gives the illusion that the present system of education—based on isms, beliefs and the worshipping of success and achievement—leads to social order
- » drives children to become stressed, indifferent and lost within
- » engenders and sustains distrust among different people across society, until cynicism and fear of one another becomes the norm

- » replaces a culture of ethics and morality with the vulgarity of the extremely rich who parade their wealth before the poor
- » leads to acute feelings of loneliness in people from all walks of life, a loneliness that can drive anyone to feel poor within and worthless
- » fosters worldwide depression to the point where individuals and groups no longer recognise their true spiritual purpose in life
- » results in a highly complex society in which the simple understanding of right human relations is replaced by the interminable, stressful and ultimately violent pursuit of human rights
- » enforces the belief that endless growth of the current economic system is needed, even when the world economy is on its knees (the same system that has already led to economic upheaval, social divisions and widespread pain and suffering)
- » causes such destruction to the earth and air that anyone who is mature about environmental issues will be seriously concerned to the point of seeing no light at the end of the tunnel.

Hence commercialisation is indeed a silent war—a war in which bombs are constantly dropped on the true meaning of education; that is, self-knowledge. It is a war that both psychologically and materially drives millions of people into poverty, and that could eventually lead to outright war between all nations.

To repeat: commerce in its own right is not dangerous, nor is capitalism. But it's the implementation of the seeds of worshipping success that sustains the process of commercialisation in a dangerous, socially divisive and destructive way. Or to put it differently: the forces of commercialisation sustain us to worship success, and we, by worshipping success, sustain the forces of commercialisation. It's a vicious circle. We need these forces in our lives to sustain our pursuit of success and achievement, and these forces need us in order to sustain themselves. And the more energy we give to the politicians around the world to glorify the powers of commercialisation, the more that disciples of the creed of market forces will be bred in governments.

But in the end, nobody wins. Even if we leave the city to lead a quiet and peaceful life in the secluded countryside, we are dividing ourselves from the rest of society and its problems. Even if we receive the best education from the most prestigious universities, the moment we leave school there are malevolent forces waiting for us, an immense tide of social pressure that is inescapable and all-pervading, and we will inevitably sink in the invisible tsunami. We can never bring about a better world so long as market forces are let loose, human consciousness is driven by profit, or young people are conditioned to worship success and achievement.

How, then, can we talk about sharing in its essence without having our eyes pointed towards the destructive effects of commercialisation? It is impossible, just as it is impossible to talk about justice without having our eyes pointed towards our brothers and sisters who are dying of hunger. How can we share when the influence of selfishness and greed has such a grip on our societies, and when we continue to worship success and achievement? Through its clever and manipulative ways of conditioning our minds, commercialisation has moulded the principle of sharing to become the miserable shadow of the poor and the helpless mother of the starving millions. In the face of these omnipresent materialistic forces, it is very normal that people will see the principle of sharing as naïve or utopian, and will think you are deluded if you say that sharing is the key to solving the world's problems.

UNITING THE PEOPLE OF THE WORLD

Originally published on sharing.org, May 2014

When millions upon millions of people unite across the world with compassion, vision and common sense, it will call upon divinity to reveal itself on earth.

At this time of economic turmoil it can be difficult to perceive for oneself how the principle of sharing is a solution to world problems, and this is especially true for many intellectuals. There are libraries of books and reports that analyse what is wrong with society, the majority of which are trying to reach the impossible—which is to propose new policy solutions to the government. A government that invariably represents and upholds the disastrous commercialisation of our political, economic and social structures.

The more intellectual and thorough our analysis, the more we become entangled in an endless examination of commercialisation and its grievous effects. We find there is no end to its web of complexity. Yet there is nothing theoretical or academic about the family that doesn't have enough food to eat, that cannot afford to see a doctor, that has no right in some countries to even debate or protest. The more we write and intellectualise, the more we criticise and contest, the more insoluble become the many crises of the world. But if further analysis is not the answer, if no book holds the solution, then what should we do?

We cannot create a better world by waging a war against the forces of commercialisation, or by trying to fight against the formidable powers that uphold the current economic system. We have gone too far now within a society led by unbridled market forces, and the interlocking crises of our civilisation leave no time for incremental reforms. The relatively few individuals and groups who do enormous work to confront these systemic issues are now fighting a lost war, so long as a vast number of ordinary people are not rallying behind them. In the same way, small breakaway communities will never be strong enough to reverse the current trajectory towards global catastrophe; the concentration of wealth and economic power into the hands of a few has become too extreme to allow a wholesale change in direction.

The one solution that remains is to unite the people of goodwill throughout the world, which is our last hope for social transformation on a planetary scale. Because as soon as people come together in a worldwide wave of peaceful protest, the principle of sharing will manifest naturally and automatically. Without this vital missing factor in modern world affairs, there is no other way out of the critical impasse that faces humanity in the short years ahead.

Sharing is inherent in every person and integral to who we are as human beings, whereas the profit-oriented values of commerce are not a part of our innate spiritual nature. The individualistic pursuit of wealth and power results from our conditioning since childhood, nurtured through our wrong education and worshipping of success and achievement. But you cannot condition someone to cooperate and share, you can only remind them of who they are. It is like the baby greyhound who instinctively runs; he doesn't have to be taught because it is in his genes, he will behave exactly like his mother. In the same way, humanity has sharing in the genes, not an inherent predisposition towards self-interest and competition.

The greed and indifference that defines our societies has been implanted and conditioned within us, generation after generation. Before a child goes to school, however, they naturally express love and sharing in their personality. This is why we have to unite the people of goodwill throughout the world in order to transform society for the benefit of everyone, because then we will recognise each other and instinctually remember who we are. The forces of commercialisation can never prevail or annihilate sharing completely unless they destroy the whole of humanity, because sharing will always remain in our DNA.

The only solution, the silver bullet, is the amazing power of the people united. Many recent popular uprisings have given us an insight into the remarkable potential of massed goodwill, but even these movements have represented only a small fraction of the world population. Much, much more of humanity has to come together without any traces of 'isms', without any political party leadership, and with the youth leading the way. All the demonstrations we have seen already were not enough; we need hundreds and hundreds of millions of people in the streets worldwide, like a planetary Occupy encampment that continues day after day—which can and must be achieved with the greatest possible urgency.

Just as the politician doesn't like it when people demonstrate because then they are threatened with losing their power and privileges, commercialisation doesn't like it when people unite around the world. It knows that when people power becomes planetary, the very structures that maintain its control over society will begin to shake. And because commercialisation is structured by an immense complexity of laws and policies, countless economic arrangements will have to be transformed as a new society gradually emerges. Over time, the entire organisation of the global economy will have to be reconstructed and simplified, until commercialisation finally abdicates its reign over the consciousness of humanity.

No other solution will work until the people of goodwill throughout the world rise up in unison together. When millions upon millions of people gather in protest from nation to nation, there is an unconscious to conscious realisation that we are one humanity. Then the principle of sharing will start to be expressed and manifested worldwide, in its infinite and varied ways. Then we can see that all the perceived differences between people are so pointless, so unnecessary. And then we can see what sharing means in action; that we don't need this, we don't need that, we just need *you and I*. People together. And that brings joy, enormous joy.

Before long, we may also see how sharing is like a Prozac pill for world depression, because in everybody there is good, a goodness that is often not expressed. When we begin to express that goodwill between each other, we feel better. We feel dignified. It gives us strength, and it gives us vision. And that is exactly what we are beginning to experience now, amidst the death and rebirth of modern society. Because the death of a society happens when that society is divided, when its people become less and less joyful, free and creative.

Millions of people around the world are calling consciously for justice, but what we are actually seeing in all these demonstrations is an unconscious call for sharing. The reason we do not recognise this *en masse* is because of the many divisions wrought into society by commercialisation and factional politics, fostering so much conflict through ideologies and beliefs, as well as so much complacency. Those who are moved by the inequities in society are seemingly compelled to engage in a battle against the system, in a fight for justice. But if we could see that only sharing can bring about that justice, then we would pursue justice in a different way through a unified call across the world for sharing.

When the heart is opened with love, it can only ever call for sharing. The heart will never go 'against' the system, only the contents of the mind can engage in such a struggle for rectifying the inequality and cruelty of our societies. In fact, the millions of people who shout for justice 'against' the system are standing for a better world in relation to their maturity, sincerity and intelligence. It requires maturity to protest for changes to the system, because when you are mature then you are responsible. And when you are responsible in relation to the many problems within our societies, then you are left with no choice but to fight for justice, because commercialisation has structured injustice into the system in such an architectural way. But when the heart and love comes with that maturity and intelligence, then the call for justice will reverse its coin and become sharing.

We are so conditioned by the system and its ideologies that we miss, by only a fraction, this experiential understanding of sharing as the means for achieving justice. What we are in fact witnessing around the world in so many mass demonstrations is the vibration of the presence of sharing within the human heart, which is becoming almost palpable—as particularly sensed and demonstrated by the youth. The revolution in Tahrir Square in early 2011, for example, beautifully expressed the vibration of sharing as a divine principle among thousands of people with different backgrounds and beliefs. It was a beautiful sight because sharing, as represented by the power of ordinary people coming together without any isms or ideologies, will always bring beauty and joy.

But what will happen to the activist today who intuitively perceives the simple truth that sharing is the means *par excellence* for achieving justice, and for ensuring the continuation of justice in perpetuity? Unfortunately, we have become so hypnotised by the need for justice in our societies that the one who stands in the street and calls for sharing is a very lonely individual. Amidst the deafening cry in every country for accountability and justice, how could anyone explain the overall vision of what they have felt and understood? It is the equivalent of saying that you have seen a flying saucer. Carry on talking about such a revelation and you will surely be advised to see a doctor in the end.

Only through a worldwide burst of compassion can the principle of sharing be gradually sustained in our societies, which is why the rise of a united voice of the people is so vitally important. Only through compassion, freedom, common sense and vision can the world's people come together with one voice, pointing in the same direction without different factions going left or right. Communism and socialism attempted to unify societies through economic forms of sharing, but both of these ideologies have failed in practice by infringing human free will. So how can the principle of sharing make it alone, without any political ideologies and without taking away our freedom? Only through a worldwide burst of compassion, like a fast-flowing river that is dammed behind a wall, until the water finally breaks through.

And what will such an outburst of compassion mean in practical terms? It will mean the beginning of the end of hunger. It will mean that the call of the people to end hunger is so urgent, so engulfing, that starvation on this earth will never be allowed to happen again. It will mean that a huge boat sets sail for new horizons, upon which the poor will travel first class. Not everyone will get on the boat to begin with, no doubt there will always be those who choose to remain the children of commercialisation. But when millions of people from different nations come together, peacefully and without political argument, the governments of the world will not know what to do. They will be left with no choice but to join in, until an emergency programme is instituted between nations to end hunger and extreme deprivation, once and for all.

The hearts of the youth are already beginning to engage in the peaceful and creative revolution that sharing can bring about. We might say that the hearts of humanity are becoming slowly awakened, although it is really a freeing of the heart that is taking place—a freeing from the stress and the effects of isms and commercialisation. As far as commercialisation is concerned, it finds it very convenient that the hearts of humanity are effectively frozen by mind conditioning. But when the public is sharing simultaneously from the heart, when millions of people are moving on the streets for an end to hunger and poverty, there will be no doubt that a heart awakening throughout humanity is taking place.

Perhaps then we will no longer see a division between the 'activist' and the rest of society, with the tourist passing by, licking ice cream, while protesters mass around the city squares. Perhaps then, with millions of people around the world calling for sharing in constant demonstrations, countless men and women who have never protested before will get involved too. Perhaps only then, through the many people of goodwill who serve in positions of authority, will we begin to see the dissolving of the laws and policies that uphold commercialisation and prevent sharing.

A true revolution cannot be based on ideologies and beliefs, but only on a recognition of the attributes of the heart fused with reason. The revolutions in the Middle East throughout 2011 were instantly recognised by each other, for example, and soon copied around the world based upon the reasoning of the heart. And when the heart and mind is fused within a vast group of people it can result in an explosion of joy, as if the soul of every individual is trying to dance among the crowds. The public officials in ties and business suits may decry these spontaneous uprisings as leaderless or unstructured, but they do not understand that the heart, by nature, expresses itself inclusively and without structure.

This is where we can observe the acute differences in worldview between the old consciousness and the new. And this is why it is imperative that we listen to and side with the voices of the youth, wherever they can be found with their banners and tents sleeping in the middle of city squares. A youth that is asking for freedom from all the isms that symbolise the past. A youth that is born equipped to envision the one humanity without any limiting ideologies or beliefs. Indeed, a youth that should be considered a great ally to the principle of sharing, because commercialisation is extremely allergic to the unconditioned minds that threaten its stranglehold on society, and the conservative powers in governments fear the idealistic youth who threaten to batter down their isms. We may think that the youth of today are somehow special or unique in how they express a newfound dynamism and creativity, but remember that the youth have always been this way. The only difference is that now their opportunity has come as the old structures are melting down, and new energies are flooding the world. This is a definitive moment in history for the youth to express their age-old longing for unity, love and brotherhood.

Now is the time for every young person to come together and demonstrate in massive numbers, collectively refusing to conform to a society that offers them no voice or even hope. They should also seize upon Article 25 of the Universal Declaration of Human Rights, and reclaim its stipulations as a law of the will of the people. Right now, that sacrosanct Declaration is lying dormant, and it should be resurrected by the public to whom it has always belonged. Most especially it should become the Declaration of the youth, for they are the ones who can take it back into the public arena of the world. Many revolutions of the past had an inspirational slogan, and the true revolutions of today should adopt Article 25 as their all-inclusive motto, goal and vision.

It will then be up to governments to render this presiding law of the people into the law of nations. First of all, a united voice of the public has to clear all the reactionary forces from governments, and then put into seats of power wise, ordinary men and women who are tuned with the people's voice, who are moving with the public's demonstrations, and who are speaking on behalf of all the human race. This fresh blood in governments will know precisely how to give structure to the public's demands for justice and freedom, and they will make sure that the visionary aspirations of the youth are guided along the right path.

In the end, we might say that the principle of sharing will implement itself in our societies through the common sense that arises when enough people's hearts and minds are fused together. When the heart is engaged, and when common sense informs our decisions, then order and structure will come about like we have never seen before. This process must begin with an uprising in every country of the world, and through a concerted call from the public for Article 25 that is received by government leaders, then implemented in economic and social policies from the top level down. The logistics of sharing resources must start from above and spread below, from the national level downwards to the public, which will represent the beginning of right relationship between people and their governments. After all, it is the government that holds the keys to a nation's resources, including the billions of dollars that are usurped by the military and other harmful spending priorities. But an effectual process of economic sharing cannot be institutionalised on a nationwide basis if it remains limited to the level of the public, such as through mass community actions or charitable endeavours. Sooner or later, therefore, the new economics of resource sharing will have to be studied and facilitated by our political representatives in the sincerest manner, and with the full support and backing of all their constituents. We can imagine the principle of sharing as a trusted advisor whom every public servant must always keep by their side, with the needs of the poorest and most excluded guiding the thinking behind every decision.

None of this should suggest that leading politicians must purposefully enact policies based on a singular interpretation of economic sharing, as a fairer distribution of resources can be brought about in a multitude of different ways. One nation may also begin cooperating with another nation in response to financial crises or out of economic necessity, but without acknowledging the word 'sharing' in their governmental policies. However, there is no prospect of genuinely sharing global resources until each nation learns what it needs and produces in surplus, and then enshrines that understanding in entirely reformed political and economic arrangements on an international level. Over time, the new order and structure that is brought about in different countries will call, step by step, for governments to meet at the United Nations and discuss cooperative solutions for world problems in line with the principle of sharing, thereby signalling the commencement of truly democratic global governance.

*

In light of the dramatic changes that lie ahead, any person who perceives sharing as an answer to our converging crises should think carefully about the meaning of redistribution. This term has rather unfortunate and controversial connotations, and can breed tension, stress and even violence if promoted in the wrong context. There is a healthy meaning of redistribution which is the result of right sharing, such as to redistribute a tonne of tomatoes from one region to another based on a system of fair and mutual exchange. But there is another meaning of redistribution, which entails forcing the affluent people in society to give up their income or wealth. That is exactly what communism tried to do, and it may inevitably involve a violent infringement of human free will.

If a government really wants to share the nation's resources it should start by dismantling the machinery of war, otherwise the finances procured by raiding the coffers of the rich are more likely to end up back in the military budget than with the poorest in society, thus supporting further warfare and reinforcing the status quo. Why weren't the richest people and corporations taxed sufficiently in the first place? Where does the money go once they are taxed—to critical social needs or perverse subsidies for large corporations? And why were the wealthy given so much opportunity for amassing their enormous fortunes, while the government was playing games with market forces and commercialisation?

It was the system that allowed the wealthy to go so far in enriching themselves, and now the disciples of the same system are trying to coerce the richest people in society to redistribute their wealth. This is an old and divisive tactic born of the factious ways of the past. Communism tried, socialism tried, and now even capitalism has joined the club. It may please the vociferous activists who blame the rich for all of society's problems, but it will never bring a solution to social injustice as long as the system itself is based on the interests of privilege and wealth.

The surest way to bring about a reversal of extreme inequality is for a bulk of humanity to demonstrate on the streets, unceasingly through day and night, and with the vision of a united world to demand: 'Enough of bailing out the banks, enough of austerity that doesn't end, enough of aimlessly trying to tax the rich—it's time to bail out the poor for a change through economic policies based on sharing, justice and common sense'. It is imperative that we look at these issues afresh with introspection and self-awareness, no longer defining our political identities just in terms of what we are against, such as capitalism or the rich.

In this way, we may perceive how the implementation of

policies based on the principle of sharing must begin with a transformation in human consciousness led by our maturity and the reasoning of the heart. That is when a new understanding of sharing may arise in our minds, which may change our whole attitude to wealth and redistribution. When the nations of the world collectively act to end poverty in its totality, then the word 'redistribution' will fall into its right place and begin to assume a different meaning. Then we may begin to think in terms of a 'just' or 'right' distribution, and we will no longer need to use the word 'fair' in relation to global economic arrangements. These are important semantics to reflect upon, because they may help us to intuit what sharing has to achieve in its proper and holistic vision. Right distribution is aligned with right human relationship, but redistribution—even with the utmost good intent—can only arise in a society that is defined by legitimated theft, institutionalised injustice, and the endemic infringement of human free will.

Imagine if there were millions of people demonstrating for sharing across the world; perhaps then, not even the rich would have to think about 'redistributing' their wealth. Nobody would need to confiscate their money from them, or coerce them into supporting an emergency programme to redistribute resources to the famished poor. A united voice of the world, all together for sharing and justice, will create such a force in society that people everywhere will follow its trend, including the billionaires. Among the wealthy are people of goodwill too, and many will come by themselves voluntarily at such a time and say: 'Here it is'. They may not want to forcibly give up their wealth, but they may certainly want to share it once their hearts meld with an overwhelming call from the public to end hunger and poverty. They will not even hear the word 'redistribution' if they are standing with the people and sharing their wealth for the cause of upholding social justice. That is the stage we have to reach, and it will mark the true revolution that only sharing can bring about.

Of course, the fair collection and redistribution of tax revenue is fundamental to just and democratic societies, and when resources are more equitably shared then there can no longer be such extremes of poverty and wealth. But in the creation of such societies we must respect the rich as well as the poor, even if many wealthy people resist the changes that are happening across the world. It may take time, but those people will eventually be left behind by the deafening cry for a new civilisation that is founded upon the principle of sharing.

*

In order to perceive for ourselves the importance of transforming society along these lines, we need to think carefully about how we interpret the meaning of sharing in political and economic terms. For example, the idea that sharing means 'to feed the hungry' is, in fact, complete nonsense. Who says it is our food to share with the hungry? Only commercialisation does, with its diabolical cleverness that conditions our minds. What do we mean when we say that this food belongs to us, while some parts of the world have no food at all?

To see the morality inside this question, we have to consider the unjust structural arrangements that have resulted in a world ridden with hunger and deprivation—the importing of food at a cheap price, the decimation of smallholder farming, the long history of theft from and exploitation of the poor. If we think 'this is my food, and I am sharing it with the hungry', it does not acknowledge or resolve the problem. How can we remain indifferent when we are told that people are starving in other countries, and then think that the food on our own plate is rightfully ours?

If we are straight and honest with ourselves, we will never think that this is our food to share. We will say: 'The food in the world belongs to everyone, therefore I want my government to change its attitude towards poverty in order to end it'. The meaning of sharing is not 'to feed the hungry', but to irrevocably end poverty through implementing justice. Sadly, in the divided world of today where feeding the hungry is a matter of international responsibility born out of emergency, an end to life-threatening poverty can only be brought about through a united voice of the people of the world.

The principle of sharing also has a tough side to its nature that is profoundly allergic to such words as charity, philanthropy and even altruism—words that have suited our collective complacency for millennia. Indeed, what is a philanthropist if not a 'somebody' with an ambitious and competitive mind who became rich by learning how to profit from an exploitative and unjust system? For how did the philanthropist make so much money, however well-intentioned and altruistic their charitable activities? As always it begins with discovering a talent for manipulating the system, or by inheriting wealth that is the product of a system based on exploitation.

How else can the executives of large corporations be given millions of dollars in salary, bonuses and severance pay, while the army of workers who keep the business running are paid the minimum wage according to the law, often in poorer countries that offer no worker benefits at all? Then the philanthropist, in order to expand his image and reputation or salve his conscience, decides to give some money back to charity. He doesn't ask the workers what should be done with that money. In effect, he makes money off the backs of the workers and gives a small portion of it away, at their expense. We should also question how there can be so much opportunity for making billions of dollars through commercialisation, while hundreds of millions of people are at risk of dying from hunger in other parts of the world. We always see the person who is making billions start to rub shoulders with the politician, and vice versa, but we never see the politician rubbing shoulders with the person dying from hunger.

If the dictionary were to give an appropriately moral definition of the word charity, it would state: 'An undignified act that results from mass human complacency'. It is undignified because we can always do something to help achieve justice, but owing to our complacency we find it more convenient to give some crumbs to the needy. And once we give enough money to charitable causes, the establishment will eventually reward us in an honours list and give us a title. Obviously, no-one should advocate for the abolition of charity, which is a critical necessity in our society when millions of people subsist in a state of dire poverty and desperation. Most people are essentially benevolent and caring, which is why we believe in giving to charity when we hear of humanitarian emergencies in near or distant countries. But why do such emergencies of biblical proportions keep repeating themselves again and again, despite all the know-how and ingenuity of humanity? Because we are also complacent, and we often give without even thinking about justice. We do not collectively demand that our governments stop these preventable emergencies once and for all, whatever their cause.

When we give to charity without thinking about justice, then the act of donating has nothing to do with sharing the resources of the world. If sharing and charity were personified and met each other on the street, sharing would say to charity: 'Who are you? I do not believe we have met before'. The very existence of charity in a world of plenty symbolises the divide that exists between the rich and the poor, the haves and the have-nots. To be sure, if governments implemented the principle of sharing on a global basis it would signify the end of days for charitable giving.

There is enough food in the world to feed everyone, enough resources to provide healthcare and housing for all, enough knowledge and technology to empower even the poorest country to meet its needs. No matter how much of the world's essential resources we collectively share with the millions living in abject poverty, there will still be more than enough to satisfy the basic needs of all. How did the affluent countries accumulate so much resources and industry in the first place? How much of the food, fuel, minerals and land in the world has our nation appropriated from the people of less industrialised countries? These are the questions we need to ask if we want to perceive for ourselves the simple logic of sharing and justice.

*

We should not accept the above propositions unless we have fully investigated the meaning and implications of sharing as a solution to the world's problems. It may seem too idealistic to believe that the key to social transformation lies with the massed goodwill of ordinary people, and that nothing will change unless people power becomes planetary. We may become slightly more aware of the possibility of changing the world situation by thinking of our own complacency, but if something inside of us has not confirmed it completely, then after a few minutes we may quickly forget and revert back to our old conditioning.

We are so influenced by our environment and bombarded by the thoughts of others that it requires a certain courage and determination to think freely and to know oneself. We are all part of the processes of commercialisation, and we are all ultimately responsible for its pernicious conditioning within our societies. Once the way of sharing is deeply confirmed within us, however, and we understand it with rage, with *passion* inside, then it will mould our character in such a way that we will never be fooled by commercialisation again. The way of sharing is universal. You and I, let's be together. Let's share what we have. It's as simple as that, and forever will be.

Intellectual theories about social change will mean nothing unless the people rise up, pushing out the old order and heralding the new. That is where the real meaning of our lives begins, and where true power resides. We may think of the powerful as those who lead huge multinational companies, who have the capital needed to raze the Amazon rainforest, and who have such control over resources that they can take over people's lives. But in spiritual terms that is not power at all, it is completely the reverse.

True power is togetherness and sharing among millions of people, which is unifying, creative and healing on a worldwide scale. Unlike the very wealthy who live only for themselves, true power in an individual sense is non-divisive and non-destructive, as distinguished by the inner qualities of humility, inclusivity, harmlessness and detachment. From a planetary or group perspective, true power also represents everything that brings about justice in society and equilibrium within the environment, thus giving energy back to creation as it is.

When all the nations come together and share the resources of the world, when humanity brings about balance in consciousness and in nature—that is the meaning of power in its truly spiritual and life-giving sense. All the so-called powerful people in our present-day society are sustained only by commerce, by laws, by ideologies and beliefs. But when we no longer bow to their authority and peacefully unite as one, then we will see what power really is.

A DISCOURSE ON BELIEFS, IDEOLOGIES AND 'ISMS'

Originally published on sharing.org, July 2014

Humanity's suffering is very ancient, and your soul has witnessed it all. Vote left, vote right, vote in the middle, and carry on voting throughout all your incarnations till you deplete your soul of Its vision of the oneness of humanity.

For once, try to vote for yourself—that is, vote for love, vote for the existence of your soul and its purpose, and therefore become the ambassador for everything that lives… for loving humanity is bathing in the love of Life itself, or the love of God as you may say.

The problems of humanity have reached such an apex that it is now critical for governments to implement the principle of sharing within and between every single country. It is critical on several counts. Firstly, to release the joy and creativity inherent in every human being that is widely suppressed through economic hardship and social breakdown, with levels of depression now reaching epidemic proportions throughout the world. Secondly, it is critical in a literal sense for the millions of men, women and children who live without adequate means for survival, and who are needlessly dying from poverty and disease with each passing day. And thirdly, the principle of sharing must be integrated into global economic policies if we are to stand a chance of averting environmental catastrophe, for the necessary time for transforming our societies is fast running out. The planet itself is sick and in a critical state of emergency, for which only sharing can provide the necessary healing and remedy.

But on all these counts we are left in a quandary, because the crucial missing factor is a collective understanding that sharing is indeed the solution to our problems, and our last remaining hope. Without an all-embracing public awareness that sharing is the only way out, it is impossible that this neglected principle can be implemented into world affairs. So the question arises: how will this awareness be brought about? What will lead a huge number of ordinary people to recognise the urgency of the world situation, and to realise that we all share the same responsibility to become socially engaged and unite together as one?

This is a very difficult question to answer given the complacency that is endemic in modern society, and the free will of humanity that means no-one can predict how future events will unfold. As reasoned in our earlier enquiry, the greatest danger in the world today is not commercialisation *per se* but our constant identification with its inner and outer manifestation, where our intelligence is led in the opposite direction from nature and spiritual evolution.[5] Thus our complacency and indifference shapes our personalities into a vulgar phenomenon amidst the extremely poor and hungry. Indeed, our wayward personalities have become a burden to Mother Earth, and even a burden to the human soul. From a distance, humanity must look like a herd that is grazing on complacency and indifference, while the benign forces of evolution silently take their natural course within the immutable laws of all the kingdoms of nature, leaving human free will to determine its own destiny. Hence the pain of every human life, the unavoidable sorrow, and the slow progress through time and space of this unfortunate planet we live in.

*

We have already investigated the malign cleverness and subtlety of commercialisation, as well as its deceptive and elusive nature that is intimately related to our complacency, both individually and collectively.[6] We might say that commercialisation has married our complacency in a figurative sense and for mysterious reasons, which causes us to remain indifferent when we hear that people are dying as a result of poverty in faraway countries. Central to our enquiry into why the principle of sharing is so overlooked in our societies is, therefore, the need to understand the relationship that exists between complacency and awareness, which could have a powerful and liberating effect on our consciousness. We have yet to fully examine how our complacency has intellectualised itself and normalised its existence, which can only be achieved through beliefs, ideologies and 'isms' in all their forms.

If we observe the movement of the mind very closely, we can perceive how the many isms that characterise every society have a great part to play in conditioning ordinary people, which in turn has led us to become confused, fearful and complacent. Most people are essentially predisposed to express goodwill towards others, but throughout human history we have been constantly led astray through our unwitting identification with beliefs and ideologies, and as a result we are all overshadowed by confusion and fear until the soul is unable to fulfil its purpose during our lifetimes. In simple and psychological terms, an ism can be described as a mental thought-form that divides and misleads us from within and without, and effectively creates a dense fog or 'glamour' within our mind that obstructs compassion from reviving the heart with its wisdom.

The isms of all kinds can have a profoundly harmful effect on our personalities. Through constant illusory and wrong identifications with beliefs, our mind conditioning eventually leads to spiritual blindness to the true reality of life. We then limit the expansion of our conscious awareness, and on a societal level we collectively hold entire nations back from evolving faster according to their respective destinies. The history of human civilisation is, from this inner perspective, really the history of isms. This is the awkward and distressing truth of our existence, because our resultant fear, confusion and complacency is a dangerous state of being that has allowed materialistic and dark forces to be created all around us, causing division and devastation down the ages to the point of our present-day planetary chaos.

We usually think of isms only in terms of major political philosophies, religious doctrines or distinctive theories or movements such as socialism, Buddhism, globalism, existentialism and so on. But isms are rarely considered a psychological factor in our consciousness that can inhibit our perception of truth and reality, and even compromise our basic ethics and morality. There are myriad ways in which isms can be expressed in every sphere of life; for this reason, an academic approach to understanding their significance will not help us, because the academic also bears a major burden of responsibility for perpetuating the isms that have ensnared us all. Moreover, few academics consider the deeper meaning and implications of isms from the viewpoint of our psychological development or spiritual evolution.

At humanity's present stage of advancement, we live and move within a planetary circus of polarising thought-forms. Just as commercialisation feeds off our desire to 'make it' and become a so-called success in modern-day society, the isms in their different forms also feed upon our mind conditioning and identification with beliefs. An ism cannot exist without a process of identification with, and attachment to, beliefs.

However, isms also play a potentially useful and healthy role in the growth of self-awareness, particularly in terms of enabling a child to develop within their newly-formed ideations. To give a simple analogy, an ism should be like the rockets on space shuttles which, upon leaving the earth's atmosphere, are discarded to enable the astronauts to enter into orbit. Similarly, an ism can help a child to grow and evolve if guided within their consciousness by a mentor, who is mindful of the fact that the ism must be let go of in the end.

The problem begins when a parent or teacher is also conditioned and attached to any number of isms, and then leads a child to carry a heavy burden of confused beliefs and ideologies into their adult life. Before long, a particular ism may become loose and uncontrolled within that individual's nascent thinking, and they may eventually cause harm by imposing their beliefs on other people. It all stems from a mere belief that we grow with, become attached to, and then identify with completely. To such an extent that, if somebody insults my ism or my 'belief in a belief', I may be so offended that I decide to fight or even kill them, as frequently happens in the context of ethnic and religious conflicts. The mind has thus become such a domineering influence that the heart is left silently waiting, helpless to overcome the stubborn delusion that has been instilled within.

An ism in its diverse expressions can therefore be understood as a kind of biological computer that is programmed with beliefs and ideologies, and implanted within the personality (via the mind) through constant identification. The principle reason that we identify with isms is to feel safe and secure in a world that is ridden with distrust, fear and uncertainty. Everyone craves psychological as well as physical security, and the great religious isms in particular can give us a needed sense of security and belonging, as well as continuity and order. There is also an element of protection in bestowing religious beliefs or old traditions upon a child.

But when a crystallised thought-form is forcefully imposed on an impressionable mind from an early age, then it is impossible for that child to put the belief in its proper place with awareness and detachment, until eventually it can be let go of. Whatever the motive of a teacher or guardian, to restrict a child's growth in conscious awareness by transmitting a harmful ism into their mind is a gross infringement of human free will. To compel a young person in our care to become a 'good Christian' or a devout follower of Judaism, for example, is to load all the centuries of pain of those religions into the poor child's mind. The intentions may be good, but the imposition of any engrained belief system can only distort a child's need for psychological security, and ultimately hinder their path to inner freedom and self-knowledge.

It is important to bear in mind that we are not trying to understand the various forms that an ism takes, such as the doctrines of Buddhism or the philosophical views that define liberalism. Rather, we are trying to grasp the deeper origins of this peculiar psychological phenomenon, and inwardly perceive for ourselves how the creation of isms has become so ubiquitous in society that they can eventually damage us emotionally and hold back the evolution of our consciousness. In every family, group or collective activity there are isms involved, some that are harmless and others that are manipulated for the purposes of power and control, especially in the fields of education, religion and politics. Everyone looks at life through an ism of one sort or another. For example, to talk of 'building character' is a form of ism, or to say 'that is just the way I am' is the neurotic expression of an ism—although everyone who lives in a society that is saturated with isms is inevitably neurotic in one way or another.

A family itself can be an ism, just as the longing to be rich or famous can be the expression of an extremely venal ism. Our very identity is an ism within a society that is so bombarded from all sides by wrong attitudes to life, that eventually isms become lodged into our personalities, our perceptions, and how we see ourselves. We even see an ism reflected back to us in the mirror when our personality is identified with self-centred glamorous beliefs, leading some people to believe that 'I am the chosen one'. Humanity is literally a factory of isms due to a multitude of factors, including a generally emotional attitude to life, ever-present mind conditioning, and a lack of inner awareness and self-knowledge. The mind has a great capacity to condition itself through believing in the beliefs of others, and it is curious to observe how the personality often wilfully induces mind conditioning in order to be accepted as part of a social group. Without exception, the fact that isms pervade everywhere around us means that we ourselves live from within these isms. It is not 'I think, therefore I am', as the philosopher said, but rather 'I believe, therefore I am.'

In sum, isms are essentially founded upon our need for psychological security and a sense of meaning, certainty and purpose. But as a result of living in a society that is permeated by endless conflicting isms and beliefs, our existence remains characterised by a deep-rooted sense of futility, confusion and anxiety. We observed that our identity or actual existence has effectually moulded itself into an ism, hence the moment-to-moment experience of 'being' in our consciousness is also infused with fear. In a society that is subjugated by innumerable isms and beliefs, it almost appears as if humanity's favourite pastime is to be anxious and afraid, albeit unconsciously and often without due reason.

We should explore for ourselves the many serious consequences that result from our constant identification with isms, which is generally an automatic process that takes places beneath our conscious awareness. It means that we predominantly live from within our mind conditioning and act on that basis, even if we think that our actions are free and not based on conformity or imitative beliefs. It means that we do not look at how things *are*, but only at how we think things *should* be. A mind that is filled with isms cannot look at the reality of life, which includes being able to live in the moment, to appreciate the beauty of life without naming it, to experience a quiescence of thought that is not constantly measuring, comparing and projecting images.

This is the unspoken tribulation of living our lives from within the conditioning of isms: it doesn't allow us to know who we truly are, because we are always doing what our conditioning tells us to do. We may not even understand what it means to 'know thyself'. So we are not in touch with our true nature, we cannot see each other as we are, and we will not *allow* each other to be who we really are. It means that many people today do not have an awareness of their inner Self, and often do not want to be alone in the quietness of that presence, because the 'I' is trapped and imprisoned by the conditioned mind. As soon as the mind is active it is caught in an endless cycle of isms and beliefs, which forces the heart to remain quiet until the mind finds balance and reason, and hopefully begins to think in common sense terms. Isms are noisy, disturbing and divisive, whereas the heart can only reveal its presence through awareness and silence.

In personal terms, isms of all kinds can lead to the denial of intelligence, creativity and self-awareness. And in broader social terms, isms can prevent the promulgation of right education and the expression of goodwill or right human relations. However, it is the dominant isms throughout human history that have caused the utmost damage and division within our societies. While we may clearly understand this from a historical perspective in relation to the great political and religious ideologies, it is much more subtle to perceive how, psychologically, it is an act of violence towards the Self to define ourselves as a communist or socialist, a leftist or libertarian, an anarchist or neoconservative, or even as a Christian, Jew, Hindu, Buddhist, Theosophist and so on. The teachings and beliefs of the various ideologies and doctrines are not to blame, and they may serve as precious guidelines that can help focus our minds upwards towards a higher understanding and purpose. But those guidelines become dangerously divisive when humanity identifies with such belief systems in their entirety, and thus turns them into an ism that opposes other isms.

The belief itself is not dangerous, only the belief *in* a belief that is sustained by wrong identification. Even to call oneself an atheist is a divisive and violent act, because the atheist cannot exist without an opposing set of beliefs in God. And where there is division there is also violence—of a psychological if not physical nature. If I call myself a Christian and you are a Muslim, there is nothing human in the division that stands between us. And even worse, we are divided in the name of a God that is merely defined by our myriad beliefs.

This may lead us to reflect upon the following question: were past and ancient wars really based on religion, or were they the result of our wrong identification with conflicting beliefs? From a worldly perspective, this is what we call human history, but from a distance it may be perceived as a most vainglorious human drama, which explains the enduring need for a Shakespeare to illuminate contemporary social affairs. Meanwhile, in the midst of all this unnecessary turmoil and tragedy, the Self is ever held hostage by impenetrable isms while helplessly observing our errant personalities from lifetime to lifetime.

*

An inward investigation of this age-old problem may help us to appreciate why the principle of sharing holds no appeal or profundity for most people at the present time, when at every turn we are stuck in a maelstrom of polarised isms and beliefs. No matter which direction you take in the arena of politics, for example, an ism will immediately be bestowed on you by one faction or another. If you are a politician who tries to bring about a fairer distribution of wealth and resources, you will soon be called a socialist. If you try to promote free education and free healthcare for all, you are likely to be called a communist. If you stay in the middle to try and please a majority of voters, others will call you a dirty capitalist. To the point that humanity exhausts itself through so much senseless wrangling and disputation, and acts like a classroom of tiresome schoolchildren.

It is not the politicians who are most responsible for our struggle against common sense and reason, however, because we hold ourselves back from social advancement by constantly identifying with the movement of political isms. We considered in our earlier enquiry how commercialisation offers us happiness in order to win our complicity in perpetuating the system,[7] and in a similar way the theatre of politics co-opts our allegiance by offering us a measure of dignity and hope. It is very dignifying for us to identify with the beliefs of a political party, and in any social revolution or partisan following there is a sense of dignity among those who say 'we are the people' or 'we know what is right'. But it is a false dignity that we uphold when our ideology is based on opposition and conflict. An ideology that is opposed to another ideology will eventually lose itself in a fight of isms and beliefs, in which humanity itself becomes the enemy.

This was certainly the case for the principles underlying communism, which were not only manipulated as a tool for infringing the free will of entire populations, but were also mobilised in opposition to another set of principles—which from the outset foreordained the downfall of the Soviet Union. The true principles of communism have, in fact, never been manifested, and have only ever vibrated within society. Capitalism is now a lonely boy who won the war of isms in the end, largely because the infringement of free will in capitalist societies is far more covert and ubiquitous. It is a very sophisticated ism in that there is no particular club for those who define themselves as 'capitalists', and it has managed to hide itself in a devious way behind the torch of liberty or the idea of individual freedom. Nonetheless, it will always cause stress within society as long as we think in terms of capitalism or socialism, left-wing or right-wing, and the very existence of these terms will inevitably bring division and consequent suffering.

From both a psychological and spiritual perspective, the moment one says 'I am a socialist' or 'I am an anti-capitalist' is the beginning of war. It is the beginning of conflict between you and I, of inner turmoil and psychological division, if not a war of actual fighting. To call yourself a socialist, or to even *think* you are opposed to the ideology of capitalism, is already the essence of conflict—for you inwardly separate yourself from the essential spiritual unity of humankind. In actuality, it is absurd for one personified ism to suggest 'we know what is best for everyone', only for an opposing ism to contest 'we have a better idea for how to organise society'. Thus all of the political isms have tried to win their battles for supremacy and yet inevitably failed, because there can never be any peace or real social progress as long as we attempt to change the world on the basis of conflict through isms. Even if the Christ Himself suddenly emerged and declared that the only future for humanity is Christian socialism, it is impossible that it could work in the best interests of everyone.

The political isms become most peculiar in their mechanism once the personality identifies with them, for they become increasingly subtle and elusive in expression after a long period of existence. By carefully observing the inner conflict that derives from our constant identification with political beliefs and ideologies, we can also begin to perceive the psychological relationship that exists between such isms and our complacency. The act of voting within a society that is riven by polarising isms is often, in truth, a foremost expression of our complacency. By analogy, when an election campaign is running and politicians are canvassing in the streets for votes, the politician can be likened to a car that will not run without petrol—the petrol in this case representing our complacency that we express through ballots. For after the election when the car crashes or breaks down completely, we blame the politician for tricking us with his promises—despite the fact that without our 'petrol' this disaster would not have happened. We believed the politician that it was a good car, hence we 'believed in a belief' and gave the politician *carte blanche* to do whatever he wanted with the vehicle. Then all most of us do when everything goes wrong is look for another car or 'ism' to put our petrol in, instead of engaging with society in a creative way to play our part in trying to heal our divided world.

In this way, the act of voting exemplifies the evasive link between isms and our complacency: I believe in a belief that is propagated by my political party, and the moment my party fails me, I automatically look for another belief to believe in. In so doing, I abdicate my responsibility for all of the problems within society, and I psychologically divide myself from you and everyone else who doesn't think in the same way as me. This sense of psychological separation eventually moulds itself into a form of complacency that hinders the expression of my creativity, uniqueness and innermost spiritual potential. Even if I become somewhat aware and stop adding my energy to the dominion of party politics, like millions of other people today and during previous generations, I'm still stuck within my complacency and set adrift in the endless commotion of propaganda and electioneering. In the meantime, the rich and powerful continue to make money behind my back and profit from the world's misery and destruction, while the rest of society fights within political isms or else remains indifferent and apathetic.

This is not to deny the very important role that free elections and the democratic process have played in humanity's evolution, but we have reached a time when the passive selection of candidates for public office is far from enough to safeguard the future of our world. If we can foresee a more enlightened economic era that is predicated on the cooperative sharing of resources, then what use would we have for mass political campaigns—at the cost of millions of dollars—to promote a socialist or capitalist candidate with a conflicting set of policy priorities? A united world that shares its wealth and resources fairly among everyone will require a new kind of politician in government who serves humanity as a whole, and who is not beholden to the present-day laws of society based on the interests of the privileged few (with immense lobbying power lurking in the background). As long as we give energy and authority to the partisan political leaders of today, humanity will continue to appear from afar as a herd that is grazing on complacency and indifference. The true expression of democracy has never existed in any country, and will never be revealed until the mass majority of people attain self-knowledge through an education on the Ageless Wisdom. It is impossible to know what democracy even means while our minds are conditioned by fear and insecurity, and while there is no trust or equality within our societies. What kind of democracy can such a society produce?

*

Ultimately, it is the non-ending psychological conflicts caused by communism, socialism, capitalism, and all the religious mess surrounding them that has created both physical and spiritual poverty, as well as the collateral damage of world hunger. This is obvious to perceive within a broken society that is being torn apart by a war of isms, as in many Middle Eastern or African countries that dominate newspaper headlines. No matter who it is that perpetrates the militarily-led destruction—Al Shabab or the Shiite militia, NATO or the CIA—it is always the poor and hungry who represent the incidental casualties. What we are more reluctant to acknowledge, however, is the part we also play in creating this collateral damage through our combined public complacency.

We may blame the government for siding with vested interests and pouring billions of dollars into the machinery of war, but the government *can* do that, has the *right* to do that, and will *continue* to do that because I shut my mouth and look away. And why do I keep my mouth shut? Because I am preoccupied with my personal conflicts within society, while isms take increasing hold of me—almost like a thief who diverts my attention so he can pickpocket my wallet, with the wallet in this case representing my common sense, goodwill and reason. I eventually become conditioned in such a way that my relationship to the reality of life is haplessly fragmented, because my perception is so clouded by isms that I cannot see reality as it is, or even have a basically moral or ethical response to the human suffering that is all around me.

Again, this is obvious to perceive in many political or religious fundamentalists, but we are less likely to acknowledge how the more subtle isms have intellectualised our complacency in order to make our illusions look real and civilised. In many spiritual groups, for example, it is common to casually discuss the millions of people who are dying from hunger and then to rationalise it as their spiritual 'karma', which unconsciously exempts our lack of concern and disregards our collective complicity. Karma is, in reality, a dynamic expression of love and freedom, and by its definition gives every person the right to live, learn and grow. This basic fact starkly illustrates how our personalities have been shaped into a vulgar phenomenon through complacency and indifference, when we would rather intellectualise the needless starvation of our brothers and sisters by even blaming it on their souls. People who like to turn ideas into isms are liable to see humanity itself as an idea, almost to the point that a child who is dying from malnutrition could be classified academically as a 'hungerist'.

The truth, if we can face it, is that to allow a person to die from hunger in a world of plenty is the greatest sin there is, and it is a sin that we all commit through our complacency on a worldwide basis. If you accept that every living being is part of what some call God, and God is evolving Life, then to allow a person to subsist in poverty is not only denying them the human right to survive, but also the *divine right to spiritually evolve*. The freedom of a soul to evolve on earth and express itself through a personality is the basis of morality, the basis of responsibility, the basis of everything that is. The end result of our identification with isms is therefore tragic to behold. We have effectively globalised our complacency and indifference; we have held back the expansion of human consciousness; and we have allowed history to repeat itself over and over again, while the intelligence of man has taken a potentially disastrous wrong turn from the benign forces of evolution.

How, then, can we bring about an awareness that sharing is the solution to humanity's problems, and our last remaining hope for rehabilitating a divided world? Even to have this conversation requires us to be open-minded and aware, otherwise there is no humanity inside our thinking but only ideology. On the one hand, we are so conditioned by the forces of commercialisation that many of us now equate profit with the common good. And on the other hand, we are so conditioned by established political thinking that most people are liable to equate sharing with the ideology of socialism or communism, until the idea of sharing resources between nations is considered 'utopianism' or plain nonsense. Can we perceive the enormity of the problem when we ourselves identify with any number of isms and beliefs—so many that, if we could look at ourselves impartially, we would be surprised and even scared? Our perception is so clouded and fragmented by isms that we hardly know what it means to have an honest and sincere response to life, thus to appreciate the freedom of being inwardly detached and aware.

So how can we leave our house and bring about our so-called revolution when we live in a society that is built upon isms, when we are not educated to serve or love humanity, and when we are not encouraged to care for one another as we care for ourselves? Am I going to help you because I am a socialist or a Christian, or because you are my brother and you need my help, because you desperately need some food and shelter? If I knew what justice really meant without any distortion through isms and beliefs, would I shout in the streets for 'my rights' and justice for myself—or would I demand justice for the dying poor and hungry of the world?

Rather incongruously, it is also due to mass public complacency that some isms are forced to come into existence, such as the environmentalist who fights for the rights of nature and future generations. If the whole of humanity was moving in tune with the need to save our planet, there would be no such thing as environmentalism; there would only be a united people's voice that embraces a simpler and more sustainable way of life. What's more, if everyone was active in transforming our world for the better there would be no concept of 'activism' and no difference between the activist and the rest of society; there would only be the one humanity in which everyone lives in service to the common good of all.

We urgently need a new kind of education that can help us to inculcate awareness and self-knowledge, which is a prodigious undertaking in a world that is not grounded in a spiritual understanding of life. To talk of right education is impossible without considering the problem of isms, of mind conditioning, of wrong identification with beliefs, and of the need for harmlessness, inner balance and freedom. Education, in the truest sense, is a dictionary of the Laws of Life that should prepare us all to evolve within our uniqueness and creativity, thereby enabling us to express the beauty of being who we truly are. Commercialisation has done its best to eliminate right education in every way, because it knows that self-knowledge represents a brick wall that it stands no chance of getting through. It is self-knowledge alone that leads to contemplation, detachment, and the overcoming of fear and psychological insecurity. Yet this is such a monumental task in a world that is overridden by isms that we have no time to reform our education systems and teach the young along the right lines, at least not before the destruction of our planet becomes irreversible. Hence the first step towards right education in our dysfunctional societies today is simply to come out of our complacency, and to become more spiritually aware.

Perhaps it may be argued that we ourselves are not to blame for the world situation, for we were all born into a culture that is spiritually blind and woefully misguided. But to inwardly experience the Self is enough to permanently change our consciousness and liberate us from mind conditioning in some measure. To know the reality of our true spiritual nature for even a moment is so powerful that its effect will always remain with us, will never be lost and will never end. We previously reasoned that the atheist cannot exist without a contesting belief in God, but even the belief in God has to be let go of eventually, to be replaced with self-knowledge and awareness of the One Life that is eternal and omnipresent.

In the long term, there can be no escape from the problem of isms until the education of humanity is fundamentally developed along these more spiritual (not *religious*) lines, whereby each person is equipped with the basic teaching and guidance needed to practise the art of living. At the same time, the entire edifice of our economy must be structurally transformed to ensure that every man, woman and child is guaranteed access to their basic needs for sustaining life. When there is a material basis for trust and security in society alongside a universal teaching in the Laws of Life, there will be no further need for people to identify with and proliferate the manifold isms in all their forms. This may suggest that humanity needs much more time to rise above the morass of conflicting ideologies and beliefs, considering the unprecedented transformation of society that is needed. Time is clearly necessary to reform all the laws and structures that maintain an unjust economic order. But, alas, within that time we are all involved in perpetuating a crime against humanity—a continuing tragedy in which thousands of people are dying each day from preventable diseases and poverty.

Herein lies the dire conundrum: we cannot blame our governments for humanity's problems when we ourselves are not aware of the urgency of the world situation, and continue to remain complacent and indifferent. The government may sustain a divisive belief, but we are more to blame for our 'belief in a belief' which leads us to remain passive in the face of appalling human suffering. Even if we ourselves are suffering from our government's harmful or neglectful policies, our complacency is such that there may be no change within our consciousness if our personal situation returns to normal. Time is therefore necessary for people to grow in awareness, but within that time appalling crimes against humanity and the earth are being perpetrated, for which we are all collectively responsible.

*

The only hope we have for implementing the principle of sharing into world affairs is for ordinary people to centre their awareness in the heart. It is the mind that misguides us by blocking the attributes of the heart through isms and conditioning, but our heart is always waiting for its moment to communicate with us. The heart cannot communicate with a conditioned mind; it can only communicate from heart to heart. And because our minds have become so intellectual and domineering, constantly trying to take us over, the heart is left helplessly silent until the mind finds balance and reason, as we have noted above. At this point, the heart is activated and speaks not verbally but through the expression of its attributes which, as anyone knows, are defined by such qualities as generosity, sharing, benevolence, empathy and of course love.

The heart doesn't think or calculate like the mind with its manipulative intentions, although it has a wisdom that is incomparable to mere intellect of whatever degree. There is not even such a thing as a 'pure' heart, despite outward appearances when we encounter a person whose outlook is not unduly polluted and conditioned. There is only one kind of heart with its intrinsic attributes. Either the heart is engaged, or it is silent. Like a new-born baby is just a baby, and cannot be considered 'bad' or 'cold', the heart is always just a heart. No doubt if we tell the successful businessman to 'just use your heart' he will dismiss us as being naïve and simpleminded, yet even he engages its attributes when falling in love, and perhaps generously shares his wealth with the object of his affection.

How strange and sad it is to observe the flippancy with which we treat the great attributes of the heart in our present-day culture, and how we likewise consider the principle of sharing to be so trivial and inconsequential. The reader will have to wait to see what happens once the hearts of humanity are activated on a global scale, because the heart cannot be mobilised through an ism that is 'against', but only on the basis of *the good of all*. All this writer can say is that at such a time, if we can envision millions of people on the streets together demanding that our governments share the resources of the world, then we will recognise the presence of soul purpose in the coalescing people's voice. And that is when isms will begin to be cancelled from the contents of our minds.

With this understanding, it is extremely important that we should not demonstrate in the streets for an idea, but rather for *who we are*. There is no political party or ism that can give a solution to our civilisational crisis, because the answer belongs to *the awakened populace in its entirety*. It is good and necessary to have ideas for reforming our political, economic and social structures, but it is the people of the world who will express those answers through an engaged heart and massed goodwill. So you cannot come along and say 'I have the solution', because only 'we' have the solution through a united people's voice. Even to come along and ask others 'what should I do?'

is to remain unaware and heedless, because there is no 'I' or personality involved in the rise of ordinary people with a single voice—there is only thinking of the group and humanity as a whole, which naturally leads to commensurate right action.

First must come the public awareness that sharing is the last resort for humanity, as expressed through a heart awakening to a global emergency of unprecedented magnitude. Only then can we foresee the implementation of that awareness through inter-governmental policies and massive civic engagement. There is no other prospect of our governments coming together in a cooperative effort to rescue the world and share resources, because they have tried every other route over hundreds of years, and nothing else has worked. We already see nations borrowing financial resources from other nations in these times of economic upheaval, so why can't governments also help each other by cooperatively pooling and redistributing food and other essential material goods? With our combined human ingenuity and rapid technological advancements, can we really not work out an international plan at the United Nations for how to help each country feed and care for all its people, and then give that reciprocal help on a permanent and structural basis without any need of profit, interest or strategic advantage?

There is no 'ism' in such economic and political arrangements if the principle of sharing is applied as the operative basis of every society, thereby freeing pressure and competition between one nation and another. The effect of implementing a process of sharing within and between nations will be to put the ideologies of capitalism and socialism in their right place, so that they can finally work in unison together. It will also enable us to look at the world's problems without the energy of being 'against', but only 'for'. And therefore it will guide us to acknowledge that capitalism is a needed tool in an innovative economy, as much as socialism is a necessary instrument for meeting the basic needs of all. Only once we have implemented such a process of sharing across the world can we perceive how this universal principle is the antidote to ancient social problems and national rivalries, for sharing also means freedom from conflict brought about by the above isms. As soon as we recognise that the interminable fight of isms and beliefs has sunken humanity to the point of evolving very slowly, we are already close to understanding how sharing the world's resources will speed the way ahead.

Hence it is imperative to intuit the energetic alignment that exists between soul purpose and the principle of sharing, which our mind conditioning and wrong identification with beliefs has clouded for millennia. To meditate on one's existence at this critical hour will enable us to realise the actuality that sharing is an intrinsic part of who we are, which will naturally inspire us once again to appreciate the beauty of being human on the ladder of evolving consciousness. Deep in our shared unconscious lies the knowledge that humanity is One, which is a truth that has remained hidden within each individuality for countless lifetimes. The principle of sharing is well equipped to transfer this fact from the unconscious to the conscious mind via the centre of the heart, which in the end will lead humanity to an amazed and humbling realisation: that we should have implemented this principle into world affairs a long, long time ago.

AN ENQUIRY INTO THE MEANING OF SHARING FOOD

Originally published on sharing.org, August 2014

In hell, people don't die of hunger but on earth they do.

Please don't let them die and let us witness what their loving souls are capable of.

In this era of culminating crises and pervasive confusion, the principle of sharing is increasingly being discussed as a solution to the manifold problems of humanity. There are many individuals and groups that now talk about the importance of sharing as a way forward for society in terms of reducing consumption, conserving resources, preventing wastage or addressing poverty, among other critical issues. But one notable recent development is a conversation on the importance of sharing in relation to food. This may concern the sharing of food through a charity, the salvaging of surplus produce from farms or supermarkets, the free distribution of food at some event or gathering, or even the sharing of a meal between friends or new acquaintances. There are also many other contexts within which this lively discussion is taking place, although the intention of our enquiry is not to analyse the various trends or characteristics of the newly emerging food sharing movements. Rather, let us see if we can investigate for ourselves, in simple common-sense terms, the profounder significance of sharing food with respect to the most urgent crisis of our time—which is arguably the prevalence of hunger worldwide.

To begin with, let's enquire into the origin of this growing appeal to share food in modern societies. What has led to a situation in which people are now talking about the need to share food in a world of plenty? When we have a family meal, do we think or say to each other: 'I am now sharing my food with you'? Of course not, no-one says that in a family because the food is for everyone to eat. A father or mother will not consciously think that they must share food with their children, and surely the children will not ask their parents to 'share' sufficient provisions with them for health and sustenance. We simply live and eat together as a normal part of our daily lives. The process is natural, automatic. So how did we come to a situation in which we determinedly say, 'Let's share food as a solution to our social problems', bearing in mind that the world produces more than enough food for everyone? Implicitly, it suggests that something is fundamentally wrong with the way we relate to each other across society.

On the one hand, you have all of the problems that plague humanity, all the terrible things that happen every day—the widespread violence and exploitation, the extremes of poverty and luxury, all of the divisions wrought into our social order. And then, in the midst of this turmoil, the idea to share our food suddenly takes hold. But if there was not such inequality in the world, and no deprivation or hunger, we may not pay any attention to the idea of sharing food. Just as a family shares its food among everyone and doesn't think twice about it, so would the family of nations share the world's plentiful produce as a matter of course, and no-one would have to mention the necessity of sharing. It would also be natural, commonsensical, and a normal part of our daily lives.

So perhaps the question is not why we need to share our food with one another, but why we have organised the world in such a way that it does not allow the food to circulate freely among everyone? Is it a matter of sharing the food that we have acquired for ourselves, or allowing everyone access to the food that is so abundantly available? There is a cruel injustice at the heart of this question. Firstly, our world denies access to food for those who have no money to pay for it, so if you are poor then you have no right to feed yourself or your family. Secondly, and most appallingly, there is such a surplus of food produced in the world that corporations will waste or destroy that food rather than allow it to circulate freely.

What, then, is the root of the problem concerning food? We might say it is the commercialisation of food, and the way in which the production, distribution and consumption of food is being manipulated in the wrong way for profit. For example, the transnational agri-businesses which control vast amounts of food have no interest in making sure that their produce is grown and distributed freely, because they are only concerned with making money. So when it comes to the poor peasant farmer who is struggling to grow his own produce, he has no rights whatsoever compared to the big and powerful corporation. If he lives in a village that can feed itself, and has done for centuries, the corporation can come along and devastate his community by building whatever it is they want to build, because the government will help them to do it. Or perhaps a foreign country such as China will purchase the land encompassing that village, then claim that the food grown on that land now belongs to them, as if that could literally be true.

So how can a poor farmer share his freely produced food among his family, when his land has been effectively stolen from him by a large foreign corporation, or by the government with its misguided policies? And what does food sharing mean for the millions of smallholder farmers in poor countries who are forced to stop selling their surplus produce to the local market, and instead export it to more affluent countries overseas for a cheap price? Do we even know how many supermarkets exist in wealthy industrialised countries that will gladly profit from that cheap food? Or how many tonnes of food they throw away each night? Perhaps the answer doesn't actually matter, because all of that food and produce belongs to *them*. The fact remains that they have no interest in sharing the earth's bounty that is freely provided by nature, or allowing the food that belongs to everyone to circulate freely.

Surely it is therefore morally and principally correct to say that food should not be commercialised, but rather put in its right place for the benefit of all humanity—not only profitmaking corporations. When food is grown purely for commercial purposes, we might say there is less food for all in a world of plenty. For there is plenty of food available in the global marketplace, but it is so expensive that there is less access to staple provisions for the majority, and too much access to a cornucopia of food for the few. So when the consumption of food is tied to a complex system of market-driven processes, it makes no sense to say that we should all share our food with one another. Who is sharing their food with whom, and to whom did that food belong in the first place? We clearly need to understand food's essential purpose for human beings before we even begin to talk about how it should be shared. We need to understand the role of food in relationship to the whole of humanity, and consequently direct the God-given essentials of life to their rightful place.

Indeed, we should fundamentally question why it is that our world is producing such a surplus of food per capita, with such spurious methods of industrial farming. Is it to feed the people? If so, then the world's food belongs to everyone—it doesn't belong to the immense grain silos where it is kept rotting in thousands of tonnes, ready to be shipped overseas for profit. To commercialise food in this way is extremely dangerous, in the same way that it is dangerous to commercialise water. By definition, the food of the world belongs to all those who need to eat it for their daily sustenance, which has nothing to do with sharing—it has to do with common sense!

Hopefully, the people who are beginning to talk about sharing in relation to food will also consider the issue in terms of justice. Remember, if we lived in a world that was equal and without poverty or deprivation, then the idea of sharing food would hold no meaning, and may never have arisen. The only reason that it makes sense to talk about sharing food is because the world is so divided, unequal and in conflict. And even then, it is only a truly principled idea if we are talking about sharing food between countries to end hunger.

The nature of the food problem in its essence could not be simpler: there's a huge surplus of food in the world. There are mountains of grains and other staples produced, and that produce has to be distributed to where it is needed for sustaining life. In a global sense, when there are millions of people who are desperately hungry in the poorest regions, we must therefore redirect food as a matter of urgency to prevent anyone dying from starvation or malnutrition.

Surely this stands to reason. Before the parents in a family feed and clothe themselves, they first make sure that their children have everything they need. This also applies by analogy to the family of nations. Before we talk about sharing food in the context of the richest countries, we must first make sure that the children in the poorest regions of the world are well fed and looked after too. We would never dream of sharing our food with friends or neighbours while our children are all alone at home, without anything to eat. So the word 'emergency' is much nearer to the problem of food than the word 'sharing'. A global food emergency infers the need for international cooperation, for effective global governance, for the food and resources of the world to be navigated by whatever means necessary—even the military services—to ensure that hunger is completely eradicated as a leading priority for all nations.

*

Let's try to be clearer about what we mean when we talk about sharing in relation to food. The art of sharing in economic terms is to direct the world's resources to where they are needed in order to end separation and deprivation in all its forms. If we are talking about sharing food, that means we cannot restrict our thinking to the level of our own country or community. We also have to think in global terms and in relation, first and foremost, to the politics of ending hunger. Otherwise the concept of sharing food is just a lofty idea that has no substance in the end. Anyway, it has happened many times before that people have come together within a community and shared food among themselves, secluded from the rest of humanity. Their experiments and sharing activities may make a difference to themselves within a collective, but mean little for anyone else.

Similarly, in Greece and Portugal and other countries that are stricken by the economic crisis, many people are now donating food to charities or to other families that don't have enough money.[8] Sharing food within communities is undoubtedly the right thing to do considering that there is an increasing problem of hunger in affluent countries too. But when is that awareness going to become planetary—not only 'I feed my neighbour', but 'I feed the world'? Now that many eurozone countries are in social turmoil we may begin to share food among ourselves, yet millions of people are dying from hunger in other parts of the world, and have done for many decades. Would we think of them, and not only our neighbours, if the economic crisis in our own countries was resolved?

It's not even a question of sharing 'our' food with the world's hungry, but of stopping the crime of starvation in a world of plenty and the ongoing theft of resources from the world's poor. It is really a question of theft, and of illegality; it should be illegal for governments to allow anyone to die for want of food that is so copiously produced. Sharing food in this respect doesn't mean that we, the people, have to personally share food with the hungry in distant regions. If somebody near to us is suffering from hunger and we share food with them, then clearly the result would be good—that person could be saved from needlessly dying. But there is more than enough food, enough boats, enough planes, enough technology in the world to ensure that food is distributed to everyone who needs it. So how does a person come to a point when they do not have enough to eat, and are incapable of providing for their family? This is the line of enquiry we need to pursue if we want to think for ourselves on this matter in terms of justice, and it can never be answered by sending food parcels from affluent households to remote countries overseas.

Broadly speaking, it appears that the emerging conversation on sharing food can go in one of two ways. We can either invent a new concept around the idea of sharing food that is limited to our own society or community. Or we can focus our attention on the understanding that food belongs to everyone, and expand our awareness to the planetary level in order to uphold a vision of the one humanity. The first way is essentially conservative and self-centred if we think only in terms of what is good for ourselves and our own country. But if we think about the necessity of sharing food globally, and if we re-educate ourselves to think in terms of what is good for the world as a whole, then the idea of sharing to end hunger holds within itself the true meaning of revolution. It will be a revolutionary explosion within our collective consciousness the day we intuit the potential of sharing on the basis of justice, on the basis of compassion, on the basis of common sense, and especially on the basis of maturity and responsibility. If we are clear on what sharing means in global terms, and if our actions are based on a revolution led by the common sense of the heart, perhaps then we can talk about the meaning of sharing in relation to food.

If we only think about sharing food on the basis of charity, however, then we will never reach the economic understandings needed to ensure freedom from want for all the world's inhabitants. When we are truly interested in making sure that every person in the world is fed, sheltered and cared for, charity is an outmoded form of thinking in our societies that has to be dissipated and eventually relegated to the past. Unless we think about sharing food in relation to justice and ending hunger, we are stripping the principle of sharing of its nobility and greater spiritual meaning. This principle also has a certain inherent dignity, so let us not degrade it with sentimentality or notions of charity. Clearly it's necessary and indeed crucial to share food on the basis of charity within a divided society that fails to guarantee everyone access to the essentials of life, but that is a very different matter from sharing the world's resources.

*

Now let us see if we can be any clearer about the meaning of justice in relation to food. When a person in our society commits a crime by killing other people, that person is sent to prison. But even that prisoner is provided with basic amenities and given enough food to eat, and is not permitted by the government to starve. That is what we call justice. And yet we have millions of people around the world who subsist from day to day in a life-threatening state of poverty, and their government does nothing for them. What social crime are these people guilty of? What kind of justice is there for *them*? Obviously, there can be no justice in a world ridden with inequity and impoverishment unless the government fulfils its duty to help all its citizens. The role of the government is to serve, and not only the people who elected it to power; its duty is to serve and protect everyone, no matter who they are and wherever they live in the world.[9]

But what does that mean for the millions of people who are blamelessly destitute or hungry? As a bare minimum, it means that even if you are poor, even if you do not have many possessions, even if you do not have enough money to fly around the world in a plane, at least you will have enough food to make sure that you are not at risk of dying from starvation or malnutrition. It means that Article 25 of the Universal

Declaration of Human Rights must become the guiding principle and law of every nation, which is almost the opposite of the current situation.[10] Even in India, the country with the highest number of undernourished people in the world, the government spends some $40bn on its military budget each year despite the fact that it isn't at war. Who is the government fighting to protect, when several thousand of the nation's children die each day due to illnesses related to poor diets? There is more than enough food produced in that country alone to feed all of its people. What's to stop the government from putting a bill through parliament that says: 'Redirect our nation's food surpluses to the hungry millions!'

Perhaps this illustrates why we will never succeed in changing the world's distorted priorities if we limit our activity to sharing food between ourselves. What we should also do is come together, unite and demonstrate in front of every government to say: 'Stop what you're doing!' But instead of collectively demanding that our governments immediately distribute food to the hungry, many of those involved in food sharing initiatives are behaving as if there's a war going on. Food is being donated, collected, salvaged and redistributed to help ensure that those who have no money at least have access to the nation's food surplus. That is a venerable thing to do, but there are no bombs being dropped on our streets or any restrictions being placed on the availability of food.

So why isn't the world's food reaching the people who need it most, despite there being more than enough to go around? The reasons are well discussed, as we alluded to above: because the price of food is being dictated by the vagaries of market forces. Because the wholesale commercialisation of food allows it to be hoarded, wasted, speculated upon for profit and sold as animal fodder to industrial feedlots. In response to the monstrous injustices that ensue from this state of affairs, are we going to feed somebody in our neighbourhood and then go home and be happy? The overwhelming extent of avoidable deaths due to hunger demands an emergency response *from the world's governments*. So the very first step towards changing this situation is to understand that we are not at war, that there is plenty of food available in the world, and it is our governments that are to blame for causing food deprivation through their reckless policies. How else can food crises of biblical proportions keep repeating themselves, again and again? The time has come when we must say: enough is enough!

It is the world's governments that have the power to change the laws, to regulate the corporations and redirect food to where it is most critically needed. Even the largest transnational agribusinesses, despite all their profit-seeking deviousness, are no match compared to a united voice of the world's people. From whichever way you look at it, the key to change is the collective power of ordinary people. If enough people unite and tell a corrupt government leader that they have to leave office, then that politician will be forced to leave, as we have seen in Egypt. And if enough people boycotted the products of giant food corporations, then those corporations would be forced to change their destructive practices that are causing poverty and perpetuating hunger. It is up to us, the everyday men and women of goodwill, to make a stand for the kind of world we want to live in. We are born to serve, we are born with compassion, we are born to help those less fortunate than ourselves, and the governments are taking that away from us with their divisive laws and policies; for how much longer are we going to conform while our brothers and sisters are dying of starvation and disease?

We have to become activists and unite no matter where we live in the world, and together we can stop this injustice. It is time for a *huge* demonstration that doesn't cease until the crisis of hunger is adequately addressed by our governments. It cannot be like the protests against the Iraq war in 2003 when millions of people amassed internationally for one weekend and then went home, permitting the politicians to carry on with their resource-grabbing stratagems. We have to carry on and on and on, in every country and capital city, until an emergency programme of food redistribution is coordinated by governments at an international level.

It will never be enough if we target our efforts at sharing food within our own localities. The critical magnitude of the situation behoves us to come together with awareness of what is happening around the world, to organise ourselves and demand from our governments that everyone is immediately fed. Even the people who are sharing food locally and those who are receiving that food should join forces, go outside and demonstrate for an irrevocable end to hunger! Without the rise of an indignant public we will never witness a re-ordering of global priorities, a massive redirection of funds to the poorest areas of the world, and a concerted restructuring of the global economy to ensure that hunger is completely abolished and never allowed to happen again.

However, let's not be tempted to believe that our existing government leaders will automatically accede to an overwhelming call from the public to end hunger. We know that the world's governments have the means to rapidly end the suffering of millions of people, but that doesn't mean it is in their best interests to do so. For instance, it is taken for granted that only strategic or economic interests will incentivise a foreign intervention in the forgotten conflict zones of Africa, let alone the prospect of enacting an intergovernmental emergency programme to rebuild those devastated regions and care for the dispossessed. And even if the political will was there for such extensive relief and support, the current methods used to help the poor in less developed nations will always remain insufficient, such as Official Development Assistance. This is the remnant of a very old and malefic system, and it's high time that institutionalised charity was replaced by an international programme of cooperative action to forever end hunger and needless deprivation.

Will our existing government leaders therefore understand what has to be done to solve poverty and social injustice, even if they are compelled to do so by world public opinion? Maybe they will immediately respond with sufficient urgency, but it is more likely that they will not. So perhaps the first step is for the public to drive out all the old politicians that uphold the status quo, and put more ordinary people with common sense into positions of influence and authority. The trained ordinary person sees the world very differently from the wealthy politician who was educated in private schools and elite universities. Common sense belongs to the ordinary people in every country because they are the ones who see the need for justice, who don't want to become a 'somebody' in the eyes of others, and who only want to serve the common good of all. They are not like the government bureaucrats who work without vision in accordance with an ideology that serves only the rich, the establishment and powerful corporations.

Indeed, one reason why common sense has never prevailed in our societies is because it has long been abducted by domineering governments and their ill-advised political leaders. Conservative heads of state are not equipped for the transformations that lie ahead, and for obvious reasons. First of all, it's not their fault, for they have not been trained to implement the policies that can feed the world's people and reverse decades of destructive commercialisation. Secondly, they would be shocked if you asked them to do so. They would say: 'Excuse me, but I have billions of dollars of contracts with foreign countries, and now you're asking me to jeopardise all those years of working for our national self-interest?!' To ask such a politician of the old order to transform his policy priorities could be a dangerous mistake, because if you carry on asking the wrong person to heed the public's demands then you will end up violently asking them. And violence has no part to play whatsoever in sharing the world's resources. That is why the old governments have to go. We should not waste our time voting for them any longer. And there is no point in protesting for those old-school politicians to completely change their worldviews, because they will never do it. So they have to *leave office*! We need them *out*!

We have to replace the doctrinaire authorities with fresh blood, with ordinary people who are here to serve humanity with gratitude, humility and wisdom. The wise ordinary person will be aware of what they are elected for, which the commercially-minded politician was never in office to do. There are many experienced people who work in non-governmental organisations (NGOs), for example, who work with an attitude of selfless service and know precisely the changes that are needed in different fields. These are the kind of people that we need to set out the policies that governments should implement. And together, those policies should be taken to the United Nations and formulated into an international program of economic restructuring and resource redistribution. The multitude of NGOs around the world are doing the work that should always have been done by our governments, such as healing the environment, feeding the hungry, tending to the poor and working out the policies that will pave the road to a better world. What the progressive and humanitarian NGOs stand for, in effect, represents the best that our governments should be aspiring to do.

So we have to get the orthodox politicians out, the trained ordinary people in, and the wisdom of the NGOs must be the guiding light of our new government administrations. Once we stop the mess being created by governments who follow the divisive rules of commercialisation, then the hungry can finally eat, the damage can slowly be undone, and the rest will follow naturally. Every nation already knows what it wants. And if we only listen to the respected thinkers in the many people's movements and activist NGOs, they will give us the needed answers.

*

In response to these assertions, many people may contest that it is too idealistic to expect a united people's voice to focus on the suffering of the abject poor. Why, for example, have we yet to see any demonstrations in our city squares for an end to poverty-induced hunger wherever it exists? This is an important question to ponder, although perhaps we already know the answer: because it's normal for there to be people dying from starvation in other parts of the world. We're used to it; it's been going on for decades.

It's easy to say what we *should* do, which is to go in unison before our governments and, with the power of millions of voices, hit hard with our simple demand, day after day in peaceful protest until something is done. But it seems the nearest thing we have right now is people swapping food, donating to charities or sharing meals in community festivities. Of the many organisations springing up around the idea of sharing food, most don't even mention the fact that people are starving in distant countries. And why not? Because it's much safer to limit the idea of sharing to the level of our own country or community. We are far less inclined to take the view that sharing has to be applied globally, because then we may have to reflect on our own lifestyles in relation to the poorest people in the world, or take a stand against our government and its destructive policies.

Even if we do know the true scale of food insecurity in poorer countries, we would rather respond to the idea of sharing in a limited and self-centred way, without stepping out of our comfort zone. We would rather have a party in the name of sharing food while millions of people are dying from hunger. We may feel good about participating in such food sharing activities, but in fact we are reducing the idea of sharing into an 'ism' or a sheer fantasy. It is really an extension of our complacency which means nothing with respect to the critical world situation, and will achieve nothing for the survival of humanity. Complacency is like water; it goes everywhere possible when disturbed, but always looks for its balance and seeks to return to the same place as before. Our complacency is the same because we are always looking for our own security, and we are all seeking a place to hide from our fear. Complacency and fear are one and the same thing, because one cannot exist without the other. We are all very scared, acting as if we will live for a thousand years even though the tensions in the world are so extreme that without drastic changes we'll soon be finished. And we are all implicated in the crisis of our civilisation. No-one is absolved from the world problems that we've together inherited and recreated, from lifetime to lifetime.

Who, then, shall we point our finger at when it comes to the atrocity of hunger? We know that governments are not interested in redistributing food to where it is most critically needed, and major corporations are causing hunger by commercialising food and marginalising the poor. But maybe we are more culpable than the governments or corporations because, due to our indifference, we do little to prevent this situation from continuing year after year.

Unfortunately, no single person or group can bring about massive demonstrations for governments to prevent food deprivation as a leading priority. Only our combined awareness can lead to a worldwide understanding that ending hunger is a moral imperative, and that it is inexcusable that anyone should die for want of food that is abundantly available. Which means that needless deaths due to hunger in a world of plenty is the final consequence of our collective complacency, and there is no escaping this brutal fact. It is not our governments, it is not the corporations, it is not a conspiracy by a secret cabal, but it is WE who are most to blame.

What can we say the principle of sharing finally means, then, in relation to food? As we have already ascertained, it means immediate action to end hunger through an international emergency programme. It means ensuring that every man, woman and child has access to the food that is available everywhere. It really is as simple as that. It is not a complicated situation, despite what the exponents of commercialisation would have us believe. What we call the system has created such division in our societies through its complex laws and policies that in the end nobody really understands what the system is anymore. But that doesn't mean we have to think about the problem of food in a complicated way, because we are all the same in our common needs as human beings. The principle of sharing when applied to food distribution will mean, at the very least, that no-one in this world dies from starvation ever again. It will mean that everyone has access to safe and nutritious food, until eventually the word 'sharing' is no longer associated with the word 'food' in our vocabulary.

The true significance of implementing the principle of sharing into world affairs is to bring balance within humanity and nature so that every person and every living thing on this earth is granted the God-given right to evolve. Therefore sharing the world's food will mean much more than eradicating hunger, because it will lead to a new global awareness about our relationship with each other and the natural world. Of course, that awareness must be reflected in deep-seated changes to governmental policies, such as unjust trade rules and perverse agricultural subsidies. Countless laws may eventually have to disappear if we are to untangle food from the complex processes of commercialisation. In the long run, we will have to learn to live more simply so that we do not produce more food than we need, or waste food unnecessarily. As long as we continually produce more and more food for the endless pursuit of profit, we are wrecking the earth for no effective purpose while failing to ensure that everyone is fed and nourished.

So the first stage of sharing food on a worldwide basis will involve the emergency redistribution of grains and other essential foodstuffs. And out of that redistributive process, a second stage will necessitate a new simplicity in our relationship to food, so that we only produce what we need and no longer harm the earth's natural processes. This in turn will clearly implicate the role of giant agri-corporations; they must also be impelled, through the unified strength of world public opinion, to pay their 'fair shares' in redistributing food while dramatically reforming their current approach to industrial farming.

All of this ultimately depends on our collective willingness to gather together and demonstrate in the streets, on and on like never before, until intergovernmental bodies and new economic arrangements ensure that everyone is guaranteed access to sufficient food. We know that we have the finances to do it, if only by redirecting our taxes that are wrongfully spent on military expenditures. We know that we have the food produce, the expertise, the capacity and all other necessary resources. So what are we waiting for? Let's unite and go before our governments to demand unprecedented action to end world hunger!

RISE UP AMERICA, RISE UP!

Originally published on sharing.org, October 2014

Let's create love havoc.

A letter to an American activist

What has caused the United States of America to sink to the depths of turmoil and confusion that it finds itself in today? This is a country that was founded upon the ideals of freedom, justice and democracy, but that has increasingly lost its way and degraded these noble concepts. Should the 'statue of Liberty Enlightening the World' really bow her head and reassemble her broken shackles, and let go her flaming torch? Perhaps those shackles represent not the end of servitude and oppression, but rather the ugly and imprisoning idea of the American Dream as it manifests in such a highly materialistic, divisive society.

Why don't most of us perceive the dangers inherent in pursuing the American Dream? Everyone understands its meaning in a general sense, in terms of the desire to be successful, rich and happy. But few of us reflect on how that dream has misled the people of America, and increasingly debased the true values of this great nation. Indeed, it is a dream that was originally built on theft from the indigenous peoples that rightfully inhabited the continent. A dream that legitimates the drive for profit through an ever-intensifying path of commercialisation—the necessary basis for fulfilling

America's desire to have a wealthy and superior way of life. The American Dream was not abducted by commercialisation, but freely given to it ever since its inception. And in that process, the Land of Liberty has become the chief proponent of a market forces ideology that it ruthlessly exported throughout the world, leading to widespread social upheaval and escalating international tensions.

From an inner or psychological perspective, the American Dream should really be perceived as a self-centred and harmful concept, in that it leads so many people to pursue wealth and success in an ever-elusive search for happiness, regardless of the consequences for others. It is a big lie that millions of young people continue to fall for, one that poses a very effective tool for the forces of commercialisation to manipulate and misguide us. For in our desire to become a 'somebody', to become ever wealthier and perhaps even famous and powerful, it is not long before our personalities are influenced by greed and indifference which inevitably suppresses our emotional intelligence. When perceived inwardly, it is greed alone that separates us from the reality of the heart and its attributes, and gradually influences us to become indifferent to the suffering or wellbeing of others. Even if we do not yearn to become rich and successful by dint of our fame or achievements, the social conditioning of the American Dream still causes us to distort our life purpose through the narrow, acquisitive and selfish pursuit of our personal happiness. Rarely does the question then occur to us: what about the others who didn't make it? Does their inability to compete mean they have no right to live in America?

The one who is heavily conditioned by the American Dream is subject to a form of mental blindness wherein they see only themselves, and not the spiritual reality of our interconnected lives among seven billion people. Their love is often crushed in such a way that they are proud to call themselves a patriotic American, even when, all around them, countless others are living in the most deprived and desperate circumstances. This pernicious conditioning also encourages children to grow up with the idea that America is the most important country in the world, leading them to enter into adulthood with little awareness of the extreme poverty and hardship that is experienced by the people of less privileged nations. It is not uncommon for those who live in the United States to have absolutely no idea where Africa is situated on a world map, let alone any notion of how devastating American foreign policy is for countless innocent people in far-away regions.

The very phrase 'American Dream' is divisive and divorced from spiritual reality, for it has sadly misguided generations of ordinary Americans from perceiving the reality of humanity's oneness and interdependency. No matter how it is defined in a dictionary, from a spiritual or moral standpoint the American Dream will always be associated with division and injustice, as evidenced in past centuries until this day. It is in fact a peculiarly self-centred idea that is only unconsciously tinted with spiritual aspiration—for if it were inspired by a truly spiritual vision then it would have been the One Humanity Dream, and nothing else. As a consequence, the American Dream has always separated itself from the highest ideal of the commons; that is, the common good of *humanity as a whole*.[11]

It is natural for the people of America to love their country and their way of life, if they find they can fit into that way of life and close their minds to the world's problems. But the American Dream of individual prosperity and happiness is not connected to reality anymore, not in light of all the crises and mass injustices that plague the earth today. To carry on repeating the Pledge of Allegiance every morning, while America fails to open her arms to the rest of the world, is really a narrow-minded and meaningless gesture in this respect. Can you imagine pledging allegiance to the flag of the United States of America with your hand on heart, while your other hand holds a copy of the Universal Declaration of Human Rights—which declares that *everyone in the world* has the right to liberty and justice, and not just Americans? How would that feel—knowing that millions of people are needlessly dying from hunger and poverty each year, while America hoards and wastes such a vast proportion of the world's resources?

The true American Dream—a dream that represents the soul of the nation as a whole—is to help and uplift the world in cooperation with other countries. That is very different from the old idea of the American Dream that has crystallised over many generations, and exists with its polar opposite in the form of socialism and communism. A true and noble concept should be inclusive and not exclusive, and yet both the capitalist and communist nations have failed to live up to their respective visions of equality and the general welfare, and have instead violated human rights on a colossal scale and instigated widespread global conflict. Despite all the pain and suffering these ideologies have caused both before and after the two World Wars, none of the major powers have learnt the necessary lesson of sacrifice and cooperative sharing for the common good of all. In the unique case of America, whose presidents still espouse their role in leading the world towards peace and prosperity, it has continually chosen to go the opposite way by pursuing an aggressive self-interest that is thinly disguised as national security.

One may argue, in its defence, that the United States has given so much in overseas aid for humanitarian causes. But by exploiting other countries through unjust trade and illegal wars, and then donating a tiny proportion of its ill-gotten gains to help alleviate the suffering that it also caused, it really assumes the role of a deceiving world philanthropist. And that aid represents utter hypocrisy when billions of dollars are given to help poor or distressed foreign countries, while millions of citizens within the United States are tragically ignored by their government. Why has America recently given a billion dollars of aid to Ukraine in Eastern Europe, for example, while it abandons the poor and marginalised people of its own in Detroit?[12] The obvious answer is that the federal government primarily serves the nation's strategic self-interests and opportunities for profit, which is the game of commercialisation that has gradually fused with the old idea of the American Dream, until both are now virtually synonymous.

For too long, America has been guided by this harmful ideology that sustains its global pursuit of profit and power, thereby damaging the lives of other nations with scant regard for its self-professed moral values. If nothing else, the sorry state of America today shows that political and business leaders need a total re-education along more spiritual lines, based on the principle of right human relationship. America has to drastically change its priorities towards itself and towards the world, so that common sense, humility and compassion become the shining hallmarks of its government and society. Yet even to state this simple truth sounds like a fantasy when most of those in positions of power are held sway by the forces of commercialisation, which makes any discussion of basic moral and spiritual values appear almost utopian.

Unless America radically changes its ways, it will soon go down a dark and dangerous alley for some time to come, one where riots, violence and all kinds of social upheaval will increasingly take place. Such is the by-product of continuing to follow an individualistic and divisive idea of progress, as evidenced in all the neurosis, hatred and crime that has long been rampant across the nation. The political process in the United States has become increasingly corrupt and profit-oriented, while its national debt is clearly unpayable—hence a terminal period of financial turmoil will inevitably erupt in the years ahead. And the prospects are dire for a nation that still trains its citizens to believe with pride in their right to achieve an extravagant level of personal wealth and material comfort, no matter what the cost in terms of environmental ruin or exploitation of poorer countries. Now that the prospect of indefinitely sustaining the American way of life has become an absurdity, many citizens across the nation are beginning to question, with a sense of deep foreboding: 'Where is the hope that our leaders vainly promised, and what is the fate that will soon befall us?'

There is no doubt that the people of goodwill throughout America must rise up in unison together, standing in peaceful opposition to the government's policies as it profits from wars and defends corporate interests, instead of helping ordinary citizens in their time of greatest need. Who is going to help Detroit now that it is bankrupt, for example? Will it be the Pentagon or the CIA, who usurp so much of the nation's income and resources? America has become like a dysfunctional family in which the children are being abused and neglected until they are eventually forced to leave home and look after themselves. In a similar way, the government in Washington is like the parent who is failing to look after all her children, namely the fifty states, many of whom like Detroit may soon fall into crisis as the economy melts. Is it not inevitable that many of these states will ultimately abandon Washington completely? For it is the people of Detroit who made Detroit, and the people of New Orleans who made New Orleans—not Washington.

*

The popular demonstrations that spread across the United States in 2011 revealed how many intelligent young people have had enough of the American Dream and all it represents, even if that awareness is felt unconsciously. Their act of demonstrating as one in peaceful protest is actually an expression of love and maturity, as well as intelligence. For in love there is freedom in the truest sense—a freedom from the old, from injustice, from the grand theft and corruption that has blighted America's profounder greatness for so many years. Those who stand in the streets and uphold the real meaning of liberty, democracy and justice are the ones who Americans should be duly proud of, instead of clinging on to a false pride in the so-called American way of life.

Many of the Occupy protesters perceived with common sense how the American Dream has misled and divided an entire nation, giving America a vulgar reputation on the global stage. They are the real heroes of the nation, the ones who should be standing on top of the Statue of Liberty and symbolically lighting her torch. They are the ones who want to live with maturity and responsibility, rather than allowing their free will to be constantly manipulated by corporations and self-serving politicians. They are the ones who are denouncing the forces of commercialisation that hide behind the American Dream, and that try to misdirect our attention by telling us what to think and what to do, instead of allowing us to live freely in the moment of now with honesty and detachment. Of course, there are many others who still strongly believe in the American Dream with a misplaced sense of pride, and who therefore looked at the tents in Zuccotti Park with bewilderment and misunderstanding, and even felt that the protesters were betraying the American way of life. But the hour is coming when all the people of America will have to ask themselves: what is the meaning of this way of life, and where is it leading us?

The government and police may believe that they have eliminated those tents from public areas, but they do not realise that they cannot eliminate all the tents that remain in the hearts of America's youth. The politicians are gravely mistaken if they believe those tents will not return, for they are already multiplying more and more, silently and gradually from heart to heart. It may seem as if nothing is happening right now, but it is foreseeable that, sooner or later, there will not be just one encampment of tents in a city park, but an entire nation of tents that cannot be dismantled by even the national guard.

Perhaps the hour is coming when the police must ask themselves what justice really means, and what is the meaning of law and order. Perhaps they should set up a special body within the Department of Justice to study the political causes of social unrest, and then tell the government to stop causing that unrest through their harmful policies and wrong priorities. For if the government is creating disorder and injustice, how can it call on the police to bring back order and stand for justice? Does it make any sense when many people on the streets are compassionate and intelligent, and out of love they leave their homes to demonstrate for justice in accordance with its true meaning? Should the police therefore continue to arrest and bully their fellow citizens who valiantly march with such goodwill, or should they turn their attention towards the government and say: enough is enough! We are human beings and not machines, and we will no longer follow your corrupt orders to stand against our own people!

For the time being, the dominant laws of commercialisation have swept away those tents and protests from our towns and city squares. But if we look carefully within ourselves, we can see that a planetary tent has begun to vibrate in our consciousness. Let us all begin constructing this planetary tent in a collaborative endeavour, building it in such a way that finally, when we look up into its dome, we can see the reflection of all the faces of every human being around the world. It is up to you, the youth of America, to show us the way by organising a non-stop demonstration in every state, until that nationwide wave of nonviolent protest eventually catches on globally.

All those groups who seek a just and sustainable society based on right relationship should quickly come together, mindful of the fact that it will take time to structure a common vision of change. Do not be discouraged by the pundits in ties and suits who speak on television about your marches and sit-ins, saying that you have no leadership or clear demands. Most of those complacent critics have no idea what is taking place in the hearts and minds of America's youth today. And it is to be expected that an inclusive call for justice and freedom cannot be structured to begin with, for the forces of commercialisation are like a powerful magnet that constantly overwhelms us and pulls us in different directions. So do not worry about how to structure your call through formal demands for new policies and institutional arrangements, but instead continue untiringly with your creative demonstrations, and in this way try to inspire the rest of the world to join you.

Through the unification of our efforts, we may also quickly realise that the principle of sharing is the master key to structuring our expression of love in society. One of the foremost attributes of this undervalued principle is to bring people together in freedom and joy, which was beautifully (if transiently) realised in the spontaneous protest movements of recent years within many cities worldwide. These huge political demonstrations, in their togetherness and joyful celebration, stood in contrast to all the 'isms' of the past and the divisive poison of commercialisation. Compared to the many violent revolutions witnessed throughout modern history, we can feel that something profoundly new has arisen. And that new factor is the releasing of the heart *en masse*, by simply allowing the heart to speak and freely express itself in unified group formation.

If we empty our minds of intellectual content and look at the world through the perception of the heart, the first thing we see is not injustice but solely a lack of love. Indeed, it is the non-expression of love in a body politic that brings about the expression of injustice in every way. And that is why the principle of sharing holds such unimaginable power. The youth of America must know that freedom has never before and never will exist without love and sharing. Today we live in such complex and commercialised societies that even love has become a wounded, sorrowful and meaningless word. And yet our lives together could be so joyful and creative if only we shared the world's resources more equitably among us all.

Thus it is imperative that we set aside some time to reflect upon the meaning of sharing in relation to the political economy and our everyday lives, for sharing is our most faithful guide to the expression of a healthy, sustainable life with justice. We are not talking about socialism, or communism, or any other political ism; we are talking about the universal principle that, when implemented into social and economic policies by our governments, can finally heal our ailing societies and solve so many of the world's problems.

Why, after all, are we demonstrating, if not for the love and joy that has been taken away from all of us? Why are we demonstrating, if not for the extremes of poverty and wealth that has divided us from one another in a world of plenty? Why are we demonstrating, if not for the ideologies and isms that are constantly thrown at us in such a polarised and demoralised society, where each day feels the same as every other day in its soullessness and anxiety? Surely the Occupy protests were not only initiated to change politics and reform the economy, but also to regain our joy of living and spiritually re-occupy our hearts. Are we simply fighting for the sake of our children and future generations, or because we yearn for something better for ourselves, too? Don't we also want to live each day afresh and new with a sense of connectedness and purpose, free from the constant stress and money-making that suppresses who we truly are?

Even from a purely practical perspective, it is strategically advantageous to unify our call for governments to implement the principle of sharing, rather than to engage in an endless fight against capitalism or the system. The youth should know that when we assume a position of anti-capitalism, we immediately fall into the mouth of the wolf that is commercialisation. The system wants us to adopt the mind-set of 'anti' and 'isms', for capitalism itself is a very clever and sophisticated ism that voraciously feeds off our opposition and antagonism. While we have the right to express anger and oppose the systemic causes of injustice, it is futile to fight against the system when the forces mobilised to defend it are so formidable and apparently within the law. The moment we oppose those forces they will immediately bring us down and humiliate us, and cunningly push us towards violence. And that violence will beget further violence, which is exactly what the system wants in order to defend and perpetuate itself.

We should therefore be very mindful of falling into this trap, and we should not even entertain the thought of being 'against' or 'anti' the corporatised system *per se*. Instead, we should work with intelligence from the heart, for this is the only place where the forces of commercialisation cannot infiltrate. It is the heart and not the idea itself that unites us, for within the wisdom of one human heart lies the wisdom of all humanity. A revolution that is instigated via ideology invariably leads to further social division and violence, but a revolution that originates via the engagement of the heart will naturally lead to common sense, togetherness, sharing and all-inclusive love. Could it be that through millions of people coming together and calling for *sharing* as the means to achieving justice, even the establishment politicians and the police will eventually come and join us?

So let's permanently gather in the streets and wisely articulate the yearning of our hearts, away from all the isms and our wrong education of the past. Let's not demand that our government restructures itself and the economy in the name of socialism, capitalism or any other ism, but rather in the name of *who we are*—that is, in the name of *we the people* who are born with an equal right to evolve with dignity, freedom and in peace. This is the shift in consciousness that is necessary to change America and the world, which can only arise in the absence of any thought of ideology or personal self-interest.

We know that all the problems in society are escalating day by day, and it is impossible to go on living as we did before. We are tired of those selfish and materialistic ways, we don't want to return to that bygone era, and besides we can no longer afford to. So let's demand a just sharing of resources and not be concerned when the politicians call us naïve, for we know that a call for sharing comes from the heart when fused with common sense and reason. Let's refuse to conform any longer to the maleficent game of commercialisation, and together let's demonstrate for a new way of life, a new world and a new dispensation.

At the same time, let's be aware that there is no such thing as an American justice, but only justice in its universal dimensions. And the concept of freedom does not represent or belong to America alone—it represents life, wherever you are, and belongs to love itself. Such has it always been, and always will be. In this way, our demands should not be confined to American national interests, which was a crucial mistake of the Occupy movement in its original manifestation. Why don't we also uphold a vision of sharing, freedom and justice for our brothers and sisters in other countries? Why say we are the 99% of all the people in America, and not the 99% of all the 7 billion people throughout the world? We have already focused on our national affairs for as long as we can remember; now it is time for us to embrace the needs of humanity as a whole. It's time to ennoble ourselves with dignity when we go out in peaceful protest, and to expand our consciousness to the planetary level through compassion and love for others.

Clearly the problems that are happening in America are also happening across the world, as reflected in the unprecedented number of mass protests that are erupting everywhere. If our common demands hail from a truly international perspective of justice and equality, we will be more encouraged to see other groups doing the same in other cities overseas, and vice versa. Together, we will galvanise each other to carry on participating in around-the-clock demonstrations, gaining more and more support. This is how the youth of America can inspire the rest of the world to join them, and how the call for sharing can rapidly grow on a worldwide scale: by upholding the concerns not just of the 300 million people in America, but of the 7-plus billion people with whom we share our planetary home.

From this understanding, we should also adopt as our slogan Article 25 of the Universal Declaration of Human Rights, for it will naturally structure our national uprisings and light the way for demonstrations in other countries. As the venerable Article states: 'Everyone has the right to a standard of living adequate for the health and well-being of himself and of his family, including food, clothing, housing, medical care and necessary social services, and the right to security in the event of unemployment, sickness, disability, widowhood, old age or other lack of livelihood in circumstances beyond his control.' Nowhere in the world are these basic rights fulfilled for everyone, and for the evident reasons we have acknowledged—including the laws that protect the interests of elite privilege and commercialisation, and the politics of international competition that effectively renounces the founding vision of the United Nations. The covert manoeuvrings of American foreign policy, alongside the self-interested geopolitical strategies of all the other major powers, represents the implicit denial of Article 25 for many millions of the world's people. Yet still the United States government shamelessly professes that it stands for global justice and human rights, while 40,000 people needlessly die every day from hunger and diseases of poverty.[13] Do they take us for fools, or shall we continue to remain silent while this daily massacre endures?

If we identify ourselves with the common good of one humanity, it is therefore appropriate that we uphold Article 25 as a slogan that represents the hearts and minds of everyone in the world. We all want peace, we all want justice, we all want a clean and safe environment; but before we ask for that peace and justice for ourselves, we want to see an irrevocable end to the blasphemy of hunger and penury in a bountiful world. It is not only a question of morality and justice, but also of intelligent strategy and common sense. We've been fighting capitalism and the system for hundreds of years, and yet the situation is getting worse and worse for the majority poor and excluded. So there is nothing to lose by changing our tactics and unifying our call for Article 25 as a universal approach for transformative social change.

We cannot underestimate the uplifting effect this will have on our societies and our collective consciousness. Never before have we witnessed vast numbers of people in the street calling for the abolition of extreme poverty through ceaseless worldwide actions of solidarity and massed goodwill. Can we envision what may happen if American activists advocate, in this way, for both national and international economic policies based on the principle of sharing? We can be sure that New York City will be full of tents and non-stop protest activity, because the poor will also join in and strengthen this burgeoning mass movement. What's more, billions of people will heed the call in other continents, from Africa and Asia to South America, because then we are talking about *their* lives too.

So let this be our resounding call: not to instigate a revolution 'against' the rotten system we live in, for this is likely to achieve nothing once our voices get lost in the interminable fighting of ideologies and isms. The system is here to stay, in one form or another, so we should rather *transform* it through a wholly inclusive demand for what is most urgent and important: the immediate guarantee of basic socioeconomic rights for every man, woman and child.

Just imagine how easily this could be achieved, if only our governments were impelled by overwhelming public pressure to completely reorder their priorities, and to work in genuine cooperation with other nations to share the resources of the world. As history has often revealed, even a handful of people can create unbelievable changes if they are in the right place at the right time, and with an idea whose time has come. And now is the time for us to breathe life once again into The Statue of Liberty Enlightening the World, until she drops her torch in protest and holds up a giant banner that reads: 'Article 25: The True American Dream!'

RISE UP, AMERICA, RISE UP!

I miss those tents and those occupiers who lifted my hopes
upwards into the light.
Where are you people?
I can still feel your pain and your aspirations.
I can still hear your voices in the heat of the night.
I miss your faces, your joy, your call for a new life. I miss you all.
Where are you people?
For you are the hope of all the world, if only you knew.

CHRISTMAS, THE SYSTEM AND I

Originally published on sharing.org, December 2013

Christmas is the dying past, but Jesus is still reborn again and again in each moment of your compassionate acts in service to others.

When you cry for someone who is dying of hunger, at that very moment Christ reveals Himself as the father of your heart.

When disappointed with our politicians and distressed by the problems within our society, we come under the impression that there is a kind of rotten system out there. Without hesitation, we criticise and blame the system. In truth, however, there is no such thing as 'the system' but only you and I in our insular and complacent way of life in which we do almost nothing to change the world situation with each passing day. The moment we look at the world and say 'what a rotten system', we misperceive the reality and create a division between ourselves and humanity's problems. How strange it is to observe the phenomenon of one's own mind separating itself from the rest of mankind, and then naming the system as something different from who we are when it is, in reality, the result of our mutual creation.

Observing the bickering politicians on television, for example, we are apt to change our voting preferences if our chosen party breaks yet another promise. Perhaps we have voted Labour for 45 years, and now that they threaten to increase our taxes we decide to switch our support to the Conservative Party that pledges to enact policies more in line with our self-interested concerns. Instead of becoming activists and uniting with others to effect real change across the world, we think mainly of ourselves and leave all the responsibility for improving society to our government, acting as if the politicians were our parents and we their dependent children. Meanwhile those politicians, in order to stay in power and appeal to the biases of individual voters, conjure up intricate schemes and profitable investments by juggling with destructive market forces that they do not understand. While we worry about our mortgages and wage a personal crusade for our private happiness, we give the ignorant politicians license to release the forces of commercialisation that have had such a devastating effect on our society, our environment and the prospects of future generations. And then we blame the system for all of the resultant social and economic turmoil, without acknowledging the part we also played in holding back the natural flow of creativity, justice, freedom and human evolution on this earth.

Why do we fail to perceive, through inner awareness, our self-appointed role in manifesting the drudgery and divisions of daily life that we like to call the system? How often we lay the blame on capitalism in particular, without realising the separation this creates in our mind which is, in itself, the very essence of an 'ism'. The act of voting is a direct expression of an ism when we abdicate our power to the politicians and then blame the system when everything goes wrong, notwithstanding our own inaction and apathy. You and I are wasting our time in talking politics about how society should be governed and structured, if all along we are creating divisions between each other on the basis of isms and opposing ideologies. It is we who create and represent the isms in all their forms, not least the political isms that we become attached to as a pretext to hide our fear, self-centredness and complacency. You are Labour;

I'm a Conservative. My government disagrees with yours; we go to war over an ideology. Both situations arise from the same level of thinking, and it is we ourselves who suffer from the psychological divisions that we have all created. And there is no escape from our joint culpability, not even by retreating to self-sufficient communities and separating ourselves physically as well as psychologically from the rest of mankind. So long as the world is dying then we will die too eventually, in one way or another.

If we look closely and perceive in psychological terms what capitalism is doing to people and the planet, and how this profit-oriented mode of social organisation became so loose and out of control, then we are left with a few basic ingredients: complacency, greed, blindness, and above all our collective arrogance. So if capitalism is rotten then we are all rotten too, because we represent the human behaviour that has sustained this iniquitous system throughout the generations. What we call capitalism in its purity no longer exists; all that we see today is the abuse of that widowed and corrupted principle, which now stands in the starkest opposition to the principle of sharing. The old idea of capitalism as taught in universities has long been disregarded, while sharing in political and economic terms is so thoroughly eclipsed that it is barely understood among the highest levels of our existing governments.

How is it possible, then, to completely change the system, when most of us would rather pursue a comfortable existence within our little boxes that we call 'my life' and 'my rights'? We think of ourselves, first and foremost, and prioritise above all else our holidays, our pensions, our entertainments and home improvements—'I do not want to be disturbed' should be the sign that we carry above our heads. That is not to say it is wrong to live humbly in comfort with nice material things, but for the rich man to live truly comfortably in this world he has to be sure that everyone else has what they need, otherwise his comfort will come at the cost of bodyguards and security fences. Even the poor are heavily conditioned to accept the injustices of our divided world, and are thereby inclined to remain ever demoralised and apathetic instead of uniting to challenge the inequalities of the system. Our complacency has been sustained for so long on an emotional level by fear and a lack of self-knowledge that it has become almost genetic. In the end, we become spiritually dead to our higher purpose and creative potential as human beings, and it is that very psychological separation between us that has caused the evolution of mankind to be so slow and painful.

From this perspective, what we call the system can be defined in simple terms as our wrong attitude to human relationships—between ourselves within our societies and among the people of different nations. If I perceive the psychological fact that society is an extension of myself and I AM the system, both in its national and international manifestations, then no longer will I proclaim 'it has always been this way' when confronted by poverty, injustice and corruption. The whole dynamic within my consciousness will fundamentally change once I recognise that no-one is absolved from humanity's problems, and at the very least I will join the demonstrations for freedom and justice that are sporadically erupting in every country.

The complacency of those who criticise the system and then do nothing to change the world situation is, in truth, a form of charlatanism. It makes no difference if we are rich or poor; a mode of living in which we seek only our personal comfort and happiness, unaware of and indifferent to the crises that threaten our world, is psychologically dangerous both for ourselves and for others. With such an attitude to life, how can we complain when market forces run riot and cause social divisions and widespread destruction? Now that commercialisation has entered our veins, our collective complacency has reached such epidemic proportions that we may have to start listening to the fanatics who speak of a coming apocalypse or Armageddon. Indeed, if this is the highest expression of civilisation that humanity can achieve, perhaps our only hope for a mass awakening to our common unity is an irrevocable downfall of the global economy.

*

There is no better illustration of our tacit complicity in sustaining the system than the celebration of Christmas, at which time we consume and consume by robbing our fragile and unfortunate earth on the high streets in the name of Jesus. How many of us recycle and assert our environmental values, and then say to hell with all our ethics come December 25th— for we must celebrate no matter what the cost. And then we fail to acknowledge that spending so much money on expensive gifts is an act of political conformity, and essentially a denial of our intelligence and freedom. Even if we don't have the money to spend, we would rather go into debt to buy presents for our friends and relatives because we have to maintain the image of a certain lifestyle. Despite the unsustainable indebtedness of millions of people and of every single nation, in both financial and ecological terms. Despite inwardly knowing the sad truth that we live psychologically separated from one another at this time of immense stress and suffering. And yet still we celebrate in the name of an elusive and bearded father sitting up there in the heavens; in the name of a happy family that enjoys the opportunity to 'see each other together again'; in the name of filling a void in our inwardly desolate and conditioned existence; and in the name of misleading our children with all those unnecessary gifts—to the extent that every child becomes a suitable candidate for a Pavlov experiment every Christmas eve. And then we fool each other by saying that it's the fault of our governments, the corporations or 'capitalism' for destroying the earth, when we ourselves are conjointly responsible for everything that is happening to our world.

This is not to condemn the festivities of Christmas or criticise the celebrations of other people, but simply to enquire with an open mind as to the reality of what is happening today. It is not to judge or point a finger because we are all to blame for the world's problems and no-one can be exempted, as we have already established. So let us ask in all sincerity: what does Christmas as we know it today have to do with love or Jesus? Let us have the courage to face this question, and then go quietly within ourselves to find an answer. What is the value of pretending to each other and to ourselves that 'life goes on' by repeating the same greetings with each passing year: 'Merry Christmas', 'Happy New Year'? How much honesty is in these words when each day is filled with fear, stress and financial insecurity to the point of suicide for many people? When most of us suffer in varying degrees from depression, loneliness, and the secret pain of living psychologically separated from one another? And when we force ourselves to send greetings cards to all our friends and relatives just so we do not appear rude and tired of it all?

Let us go further and enquire why at Christmas time we kill so many millions of animals and cut down so many trees in the name of a spurious Christmas spirit, only so that we may enjoy our festive dinner with laughter and indifference to what is happening in the world beyond our table. So much of the resources of the earth are therefore destroyed and wasted in order for us to fill a hole in our anxious and empty existence, as if the love of Jesus only vibrated in our homes every December 25th. At the end of the day, all of this destruction and self-indulgence is enacted for no truly moral purpose but for the sake of a mere belief—a belief that the church, in its labyrinth of distorted creeds, has misled us in for millennia.

We may say to ourselves that buying so many gifts is an expression of our love and affection, but why does that love have to be expressed chronologically on a specified date? Is it really love, or conformity and conditioning based on the denial of our intelligence and a 'belief in a belief'? In which case, our herd-like purchasing of presents, fir trees and so much food and drink is a social act that is inherently devoid of love and freedom, and inevitably characterised by mental or spiritual discomfort—because conformity cannot exist without its roots in fear. Our excessive consumption is automatic and hence unthinking in its violence toward this earth and toward ourselves. It is an unconscious lie that perpetuates the very system we profess to dislike, while habitually diverting our attention away from our collective complicity, hypocrisy and complacency.

Remember that we are all part of this reality, and we are all charlatans to some degree by dint of even participating in our present-day society. And celebrating Christmas is not a crime, so let's look at ourselves without condemnation but with all humility. Let's try to be aware of what we're doing and realise the fact that we constitute the very system we abhor, even though we do not want to see the part we play in creating this malignant social order. Together let's observe the interdependence of everything that is happening in the world, and ask if we can celebrate Christmas in a different and truly loving way.

Because it is not the love of Christ that is guiding our festivities, but rather the forces of commercialisation that are feasting on our conditioning and conformity. That is the truth of what is really going on, as anyone who has observed the queues of desperate shoppers in holiday sales can attest to. The multinational corporations are feasting on our conditioned compulsion to buy and buy, while the banks are feasting on our social conformity that pushes us ever deeper into debt. And when the whole system of unsustainable borrowing and lending implodes, it may be the governments that bail out reckless banks to try and resuscitate a melting economy, but it is WE who seek to continue with a supposed normal way of life, who quickly return to our same self-interested behaviours as before, and who thereby willingly sustain this iniquitous system. The world situation is so insecure that very soon there can be no more bailouts, either for the rich or the poor. And yet STILL we celebrate come December 25th, which has absolutely nothing to do with Christ or what He said.

We are all familiar with the words of Jesus on the cross: 'My God, my God, why have you forsaken me?' (ēlî ēlî lamâ azavtanî). But today it's as if humanity is silently and unconsciously saying: 'My God, why have we forsaken YOU by allowing commercialisation to dominate our lives, thus desecrating your holy kingdom and renouncing your teaching on right human relations?'

The reality is that December 25th is a sad and terrible day, because at this time when we are celebrating the birth of Christ, many millions of men, women and children are deprived of the basic necessities of life, let alone the luxury of a Christmas banquet. And at the stroke of midnight on January 1st, we wish each other a happy new year at the precise moment that thousands of our brothers and sisters are near to dying in distant countries. It is almost as if we are celebrating those needless deaths from hunger, malnutrition and disease. We may still protest that it has always been this way, but would we gaily celebrate Christmas and New Year's Eve if someone had died within our family, God forbid? Why, then, do we do nothing as thousands of people die each day from avoidable poverty-related causes, and think nothing of it? In such times as these, what we are in fact celebrating is our self-proclaimed freedom to remain complacent, oblivious and immature behind an age-old alibi that says 'life is short', 'you only live once', or 'let's meet up and have a good time'.

As an experiment on just one New Year's Eve, try not to do anything that evening and instead stay at home alone, without watching television or communicating with anyone. And then see how lonely you feel at midnight, in the knowledge that everyone outside is revelling and having fun. At that moment, imagine you are suffering from acute hunger and have no prospect of obtaining food, while the rest of the world is blithely continuing with their new year celebrations. Let us try to imagine: how would that feel?

However dramatic it may seem, the fact remains that our complacency on a collective and worldwide scale is so dangerous that it kills other people. Our complacency kills the poor either directly or indirectly; but it also slowly kills ourselves in a spiritual and moral sense as we continue to pursue a way of life that is divided from the rest of humanity. We all know that people are dying from poverty somewhere in the world, but how many of us do anything about it? Only the very few. In which case there is no moral distinction between our own celebrations at Christmas and the mafia family that kills many people, and then attends church on Christmas day in the memory of Jesus and His message. Of course, it is natural to enjoy and participate in traditional social festivities, but what kind of enjoyment can there be while millions of poor parents are witnessing, in their own arms, their child dying of undernutrition? And while so much food and other essential resources are shamelessly wasted and not shared with those in desperate need?

When our festivities are over and we read the daily newspapers, we are often disgusted when a billionaire builds an enormous palace in the vicinity of slum settlements or in a very poor neighbourhood. But why don't we acknowledge that we all live in precisely the same way on a global or cross-societal basis? Are we not ashamed, or is our complacency so culturally ingrained that we have now become totally indifferent?

Please reflect on this for yourself, and try to objectively perceive how our individual complacency, our family's complacency and our nation's complacency has continued for so many years that having poor people dying from hunger around the world has become the norm. It is a planetary complacency which effectively says: 'It is their destiny to perish in poverty, and it has got nothing to do with me'. Our governments do nothing to stop thousands of people from needlessly dying every day, because we allow them to get away with it. So we are the system too, and the system is us: everything is interconnected. So long as the ordinary person moves within a life of indifference, so long as 'I' do nothing to raise my voice for justice, then all of the bankers and the big corporations cannot be blamed for making money amidst widespread misery and destruction.

For how long are we going to play deaf and dumb, refusing to listen to the cries of the suffering millions or even talk about these issues to our families and friends? For how long are we going to bow to the authority of politicians with their obscure policies, thus allowing the forces of commercialisation to abduct our children from our love and affection? For how long are we going to remain conditioned by the rules of isms that tell us what to do, which way to go, how to be happy and who to vote for? And for how long are we going to remain so frightened and asleep, denying ourselves the freedom to live each day as a new day? Surely the time has finally come to stop repressing who we truly are—that is, the compassionate and caring human beings that we are born to be!

We all know those very personal moments when we are alone at home, sitting on our bed and gazing at the floor. Reflecting on our lives, we think of the futility that is involved in working so hard to pay the rent or mortgage, with the constant uncertainty and worry of losing our jobs or homes. We think of all the buried pain within ourselves, the short-lived moments of contentment and the ever-present but unspoken loneliness. The rare kindnesses we have received and all the tears we have shed. The ceaseless longing to be happy and to be loved. The desperate yearning to find the right partner; the eventual marriage; the heartrending divorce. The unnecessary and stressful image that we must maintain to be accepted in a judgemental, insincere and covetous society. The anxiety that torments us in dreams, and the fear of becoming old and unwanted. And the television that shows again and again the same politicians, the same dull faces and the countless trivial programmes. Sitting on that bed with a hopeless view of our relationship with the world, we are liable to wonder how society has made us so indifferent to each other's suffering. And how the system has managed to diminish our compassion for all that lives, while disconnecting us from our children and from nature, and depleting the little love that is left in our hearts. We all know those moments when we feel angry, guilty and worthless, when emptiness and despair overwhelms our thoughts, and when we finally decide to switch off the lights and cover our heads with the blanket, silently wondering: there must be more to life than this!

*

In light of all the suffering and critical problems in the world, what better way to celebrate Christmas this year than to go out in the streets and peacefully demonstrate for an end to poverty and injustice. To say: no more cutting trees! No more buying extravagant presents! And then to raise our voices for all the world's people to be fed, cared for and nourished. Wouldn't that be the best Christmas we have ever known? Because then we would not only express our loyalty and affection for our own family and friends, but we would also stand in loving unity with the entire world. If Jesus were walking among us today, perhaps that is what He would call on us to do. He would not want us to continue with our indulgent festivities that have no essence of true love in them. The very least we could do in His memory is organise meetings for how to help the poor, and then think of the needs of others and of the environment.

For example, if for only one year we could abstain from celebrating Christmas and new year with massive spending and overconsumption, think of what could be done with all the money we would save for our brothers and sisters who are dying of hunger and disease. Imagine what we could overcome together if all of that money were pooled and redistributed to those who urgently need it, and the kind of Christmas that would be. Imagine how our children would cry out of love in the midst of an explosion of world goodwill. And think of the power of that love and freedom expressed in every country, with millions of people united under the banner of one humanity—free from beliefs, free from authority, and free to express the dignity and beauty of being who we truly are. Perhaps then we would experience the ever-simple presence of the Christ, among us again at long last.

We are not talking about sending more parcels to the poor for the sake of charity at Christmas, which has no relation to the psychological and spiritual revolution that we are here imagining in human terms. It is high time we eliminated the conditioning of charity from our minds, for it is such an undignified way to look at love. It is also insulting to both the giver and receiver, if after giving we continue with our complacent way of life instead of helping the poor to achieve justice, or in any way changing society and our own consciousness. And the poor will say nothing because they rarely do, especially in the most impoverished countries where all they know is to die of hunger. We may donate to charitable causes at Christmas, and that is a necessary thing to do, but then we will act as if nothing has happened and soon forget about our chosen cause. Hence we normalise poverty and social injustice, and we ourselves become part of the reason why such inequality and suffering endures.

So instead of sending more of our parcels to the poor, let's unite and demand that our governments end poverty once and for all—not through the means of condescending charity, but by redistributing our nation's surplus resources in the name of justice and right human relations. Let's unite in our hundreds of thousands on the streets of every city, and demand that our governments make an inventory of everything we have and do not need, and compare it with the requirements of other nations. This is not an unusual thing to ask for; when moving home, every family is used to taking stock of everything it has in order to find out what it doesn't need, and much is then donated to charity. Now let's ask that every government make its own inventory of the nation's excess resources, and works out, through the United Nations, the logistics for how to redistribute those surpluses to the world regions most in need.

We cannot deem this charity if it is instituted through new intergovernmental arrangements that ensure, in perpetuity, the elimination of life-threatening deprivation and preventable disease. Many countries are producing far in excess of what they need, especially in terms of grains and other essential food produce; so it is not much to ask that the family of nations make a global inventory of all that is produced in surfeit, and then cooperate to share the world's resources and finally eradicate extreme poverty. And if our government refuses to do it, let's stand in the street in such vast numbers that the overwhelming power of the people's voice will bring the right politicians into office, those well equipped to serve the rising call for freedom, equality and justice.

None of this is to suggest that we should not celebrate Christmas, so long as we continue this tradition in a more humble and loving way towards each other and towards the earth. We cannot commemorate the birth of Christ through a conditioned mind, and without any moral consideration about what is happening today. Nor can we consider Christmas to be a religious observance if we are only concerned with food, drink, presents and laughter, while disregarding the grave problems of the world and not even mentioning the words Jesus, poverty or injustice. Let's take our drinks and organise a mass demonstration in the streets, at the very least, and forget about the tinsel decorations and roasted turkey.

And if we would like to remember Jesus, let's share food within our homes in a very modest manner and without the costly gifts, the usual gluttony, or the commercialism and gross materialism that denigrates this supposed holy time of year. In its place, let's use Christmas day as an opportunity to practise right human relations among our family and friends, and demonstrate love in action by serving each other during the brief holiday time we spend together. This will bring us closer to the memory of Jesus than any ritual performed in His name. There is no doubt it would have a great effect on our children in particular, and help bring us all to awareness of the Christ's simple teaching.

If we want to experience the presence and energy of Christ at Christmas time, it will never happen if we sit around in idle chatter while overeating and getting drunk. Because the true nature of the Christ is unconditional love and self-sacrificing service, as anyone knows. Many people are waiting for a great day of declaration to take place when the Christ will return to the everyday affairs of men, but we forget that there are countless declarations of the Christ's presence that are already happening every day and all around us. When you experience joy in seeing someone you cherish in your life after many years of absence, that is a declaration of the Christ and His love. When a critically injured man is saved by Doctors Without Borders in a war zone, the energy of the Christ is there when the man, once healed, gratefully clasps the hand of his foreign doctor. Or if you have fed someone who is destitute and hungry, and then witnessed the look of thankfulness in that person's eye as they are eating, that is a pronouncement of the Christ's presence among two people.

Can we therefore envision what a great planetary event it will be when we unite on the streets for freedom and justice, when we finally recognise the Christ Principle within each other and ourselves, and when we unitedly call upon our governments to share the resources of the world? Can we even conceive of such a display of compassion for one another, where there is no longer any division between the people of every nation but only the one love? We think of Christ as the Lord of Love, a one-time visitor to the world of men sent to awaken that principle within us, but if you truly express love for other people then you are also free, both inwardly and outwardly. The interconnection between love and freedom is very intimate and real, hence if the Christ is the embodiment of love then He is also the Lord of Freedom. So if we want to know the true nature of the Christ this Christmas, let's unite in demonstrations and make a stand for a new dispensation, a new earth and a new revelation, and together let's experience what may happen.

Please take a moment, shut your eyes and imagine that you are the Christ. Looking out into the world with its depths of suffering, injustice and chaos, you decide to return and release your teaching once again. How would you start your work knowing that man has sunken into a deep ocean of beliefs and complexity, where simplicity is almost non-existent, and mind conditioning has reached its peak? Knowing also the immense opposition that is waiting to persecute you with rage and hostility, and that before you walk again among everyday society a voice from heaven will whisper: 'My Son, remember that the infringement of human free will is forbidden.' Furthermore, obscure powers are waiting to engage you in a very tricky game of chess, an inscrutable contest made especially for you by the prevailing forces of commercialisation. And those forces know, all too well, that the Kings and Queens in this game are made not of wood but of human free will. How would you go about helping this unfortunate world, and where would you begin?

We may ask what role the church has to play in confronting this reality, and whether the priests would even recognise the Christ if He were walking among us today. Or perhaps more pertinently, we may ask if Jesus would recognise His church and what it has become. The church leaders of today seem more preoccupied with recruiting believers in a fabled God than following the Christ's simple instruction to serve and help the poor. Or else they appear engrossed in arcane theological debates about what Jesus *might* have said all those years ago, a figurehead that they have placed somewhere 'up there' in a mythical heaven and removed from our everyday world. They are not training their flock to go out in the streets and do something for justice, thus perceiving the grave reality of commercialisation and the crying need for a unified voice of the world's people. Instead, they preach about a historical figure called Jesus as if He were not Jesus anymore—that is, a man who radically disrupted the status quo by inspiring us to love our neighbours as ourselves.

We have prayed to Christ for two thousand years: is that not enough? We have built thousands of wonderful temples in his glory: is that not enough? Isn't it time to forget our ceremonies and worship and finally recognise the Christ in each other and within ourselves, united under the banner that reads 'freedom and justice for all'? Isn't it time for the priest to put his regalia aside and join our cries in the streets for sharing, peace and an end to hunger? We may ask: where were the priests when capital cities were covered by hundreds of tents and protesters? Where is the groundswell of popular support among the clergy now that Pope Francis has made a stand for economic reform and global equality? And who are the true priests in modern society if we consider the earth as God's holy temple—is it the clerics who occupy their time with rituals and vain confessions, or is it the activists for Greenpeace and thousands of other groups who fight to defend and uphold the rights of Mother Nature?

The role of the church is to heal, guide, protect, teach and bring awareness, but it seems as if ordinary engaged citizens are doing this job in place of the church overall. Hence the only way for the church to reform itself in line with the teachings of Jesus is to stand by the emerging people's voice—like many religious campaigners are trying to do, despite widespread resistance from within their ministries. If the Christian and Catholic churches remain distorted in their understanding of divinity and the Christ, it is inevitable that they will be increasingly left behind, as already evidenced by the many old church buildings that are closed for worship and put up for sale. But if the church perceives the love and presence of Christ in peaceful mass protests throughout the world, and if it moves in unison with public opinion for more free and tolerant nations, then it has an important role to play in the great social transformation that lies ahead.

It is the responsibility of us all, regardless of our colour or creed or position in this life, to participate in creating that unified call for justice, to recognise the malefic effects of a culture in thrall to commercialisation, and to raise our voice toward our governments along with millions of other people. Once these events begin to take place, it won't be long before the principle of sharing is recognised as the last and only solution to world problems.

Endnotes

1 The statistic of 1.4 billion people struggling to survive on less than US$1.25 a day was correct when this article was originally written in late 2011. According to the World Bank, 734 million people now live below an adjusted poverty line of $1.90 a day, or 10 percent of the world's population. However, these figures are long criticised on many counts, not least for failing to reflect how much financial income is needed to fulfil the right to "a standard of living adequate for... health and well-being" (Universal Declaration of Human Rights, Article 25.1). More than 40 percent of humanity lives on less than $5.50 a day, for example, including some 90 percent of the population in South Asia and sub-Saharan Africa. A multidimensional view of poverty—wherein other aspects of deprivation are included, such as access to basic utilities, healthcare, education and security—reveals a more alarming truth:

that the vast majority of all people in the developing world still live without sufficient means for a healthy and dignified life. To learn more on these issues, visit www.sharing.org

2   This refers to the 2011 military intervention in Libya led by the United States and its NATO allies, ostensibly to protect civilians in response to events during the Libyan Civil War. The operation ended in late October 2011 following the capture and death of Libya's deposed leader, Muammar al-Qaddafi.

3   In 2011, a severe drought affected East Africa which led to a food crisis across the entire region. The greatest emergency was in southern Somalia, an area then under the control of the Islamic militant group al-Shabab. Many international aid organisations and UN agencies were driven out, while those remaining were often forced to pay illegal bribes, endure attacks on staff and accept the diversion of food supplies to fighters. Half of the population of Somalia were faced with starvation during the height of the crisis, which eventually claimed over 250,000 lives.

4   Article 25 of the Universal Declaration of Human Rights (General Assembly resolution 217 A): (1) Everyone has the right to a standard of living adequate for the health and well-being of himself and of his family, including food, clothing, housing and medical care and necessary social services, and the right to security in the event of unemployment, sickness, disability, widowhood, old age or other lack of livelihood in circumstances beyond his control. (2) Motherhood and childhood are entitled to special care and assistance. All children, whether born in or out of wedlock, shall enjoy the same social protection.

5   See the previous article 'Commercialisation: the antithesis of sharing'.
6   Ibid.
7   Ibid.
8   These observations were made in the wake of the European sovereign debt crisis, which peaked between 2010 and 2012.
9   Such a statement may sound controversial, but it is in fact the basis of international human rights law. All governments have recognised their duty to respect, protect and fulfil human rights obligations not only within their own borders, but also extraterritorially. This commitment is captured in the Charter of the United Nations, the Universal Declaration of Human Rights and numerous other international treaties. For more information, see the *Maastricht Principles on Extraterritorial Obligations of States in the Area of Economic, Social and Cultural Rights*.
10 See note 4.
11 cf. Mohammed Sofiane Mesbahi, *The Commons of Humanity*, Share The World's Resources, 2017.
12 The example of Ukraine was relevant at the time of writing in 2014 following the crisis across the region that led to mass protests and the violent ousting of then-president, Viktor Yanukovych. The political conflict was manipulated by the United States and other European powers that had a longstanding interest in supporting a pro-Western government in Ukraine. The mentioning of Detroit in the United States was also significant because, during that same period, it filed the largest municipal bankruptcy in U.S. history. The city of Detroit was then renowned for its major economic and demographic decline, severe urban

decay and widespread poverty (proportionally the highest among all 71 U.S. cities).

13 This figure may seem questionably large, but it in fact probably underestimates the amount of people who needlessly die each day as a result of extreme poverty and inadequate social protection. The calculation was originally based on 'Disease burden and mortality estimates' from the World Health Organisation in 2012. Only communicable, maternal, perinatal, and nutritional diseases were considered for the analysis, referred to as 'Group I' causes by the WHO. Ninety six percent of all deaths from these causes occur in low- and middle-income countries and are considered largely preventable. Yet the true extent of life-threatening deprivation worldwide—largely ignored by the mainstream media—is set to increase considerably as a result of the coronavirus pandemic since early 2020. As this book goes to press, the United Nations already estimates that an additional 130 million people living in conflict-scarred nations are being pushed to the brink of starvation.

ABOUT THE AUTHOR

Mohammed Sofiane Mesbahi is the founder of Share The World's Resources (STWR), a civil society organisation based in London, UK, with consultative status at the Economic and Social Council of the United Nations. STWR is a not-for-profit organisation registered in England, no. 4854864.

For more information about STWR, please visit www.sharing.org

Editorial assistance: Adam W. Parsons.